Pictures of
The West Cornwall Coastline

The South West Coast Path
from
Portreath to Falmouth

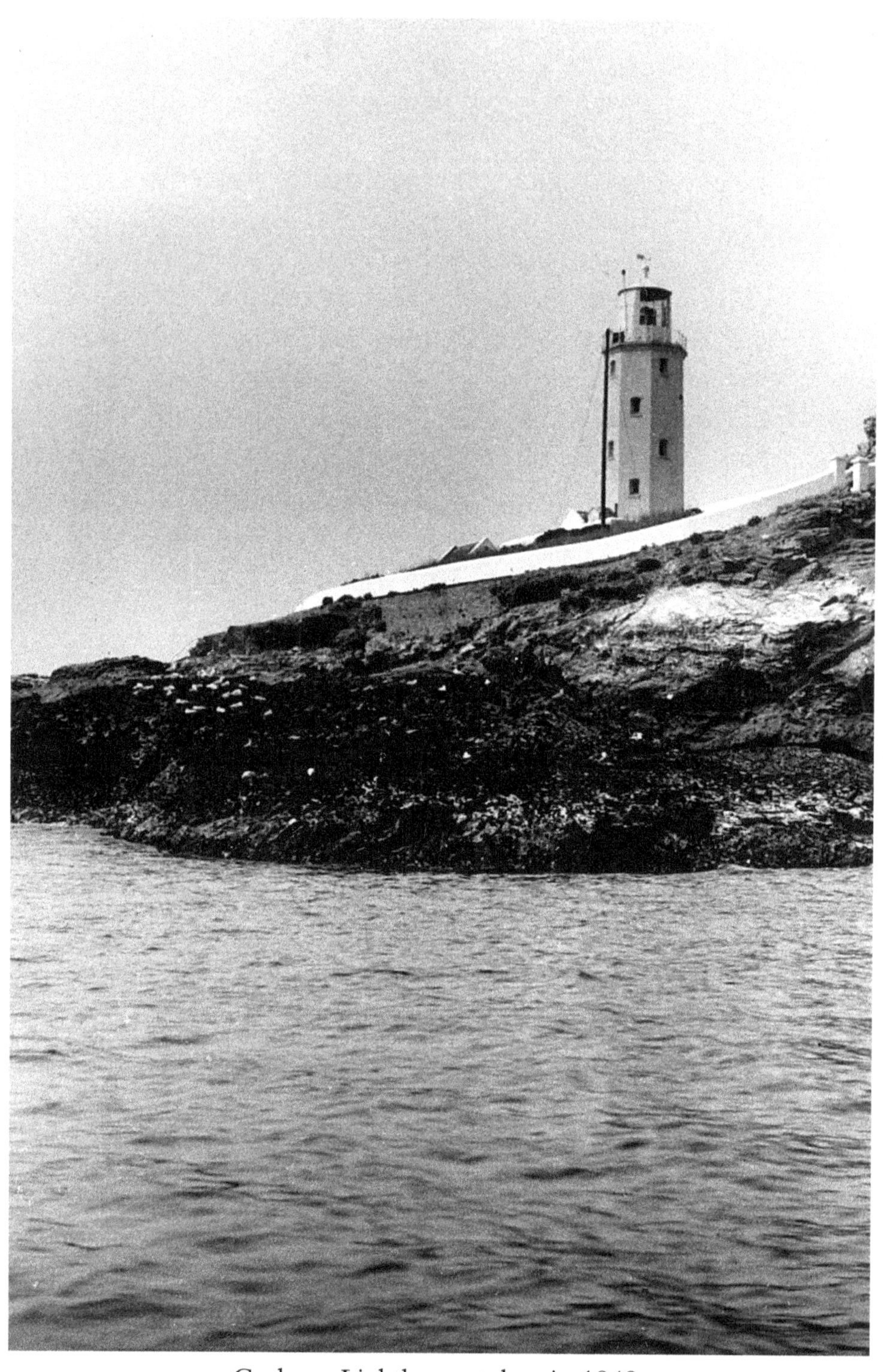

Godrevy Lighthouse, taken in 1949.

Pictures of The West Cornwall Coastline

The South West Coast Path from Portreath to Falmouth

SVP

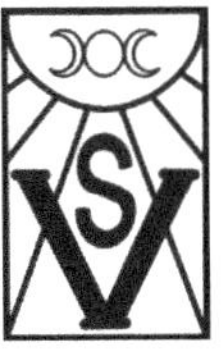

Published by S.V.P

ISBN 978-1-7392934-1-3

To Claire Morgan..

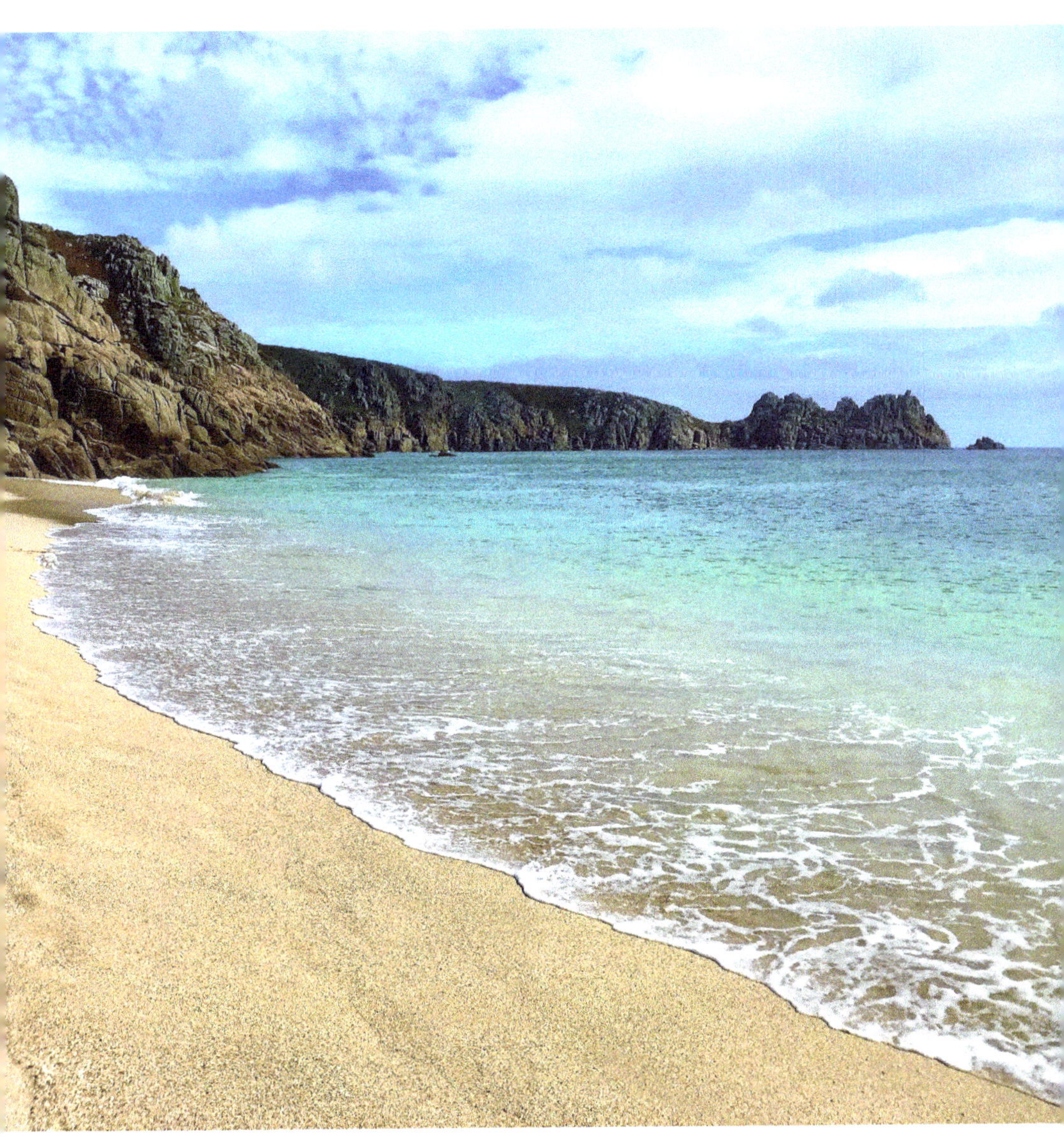

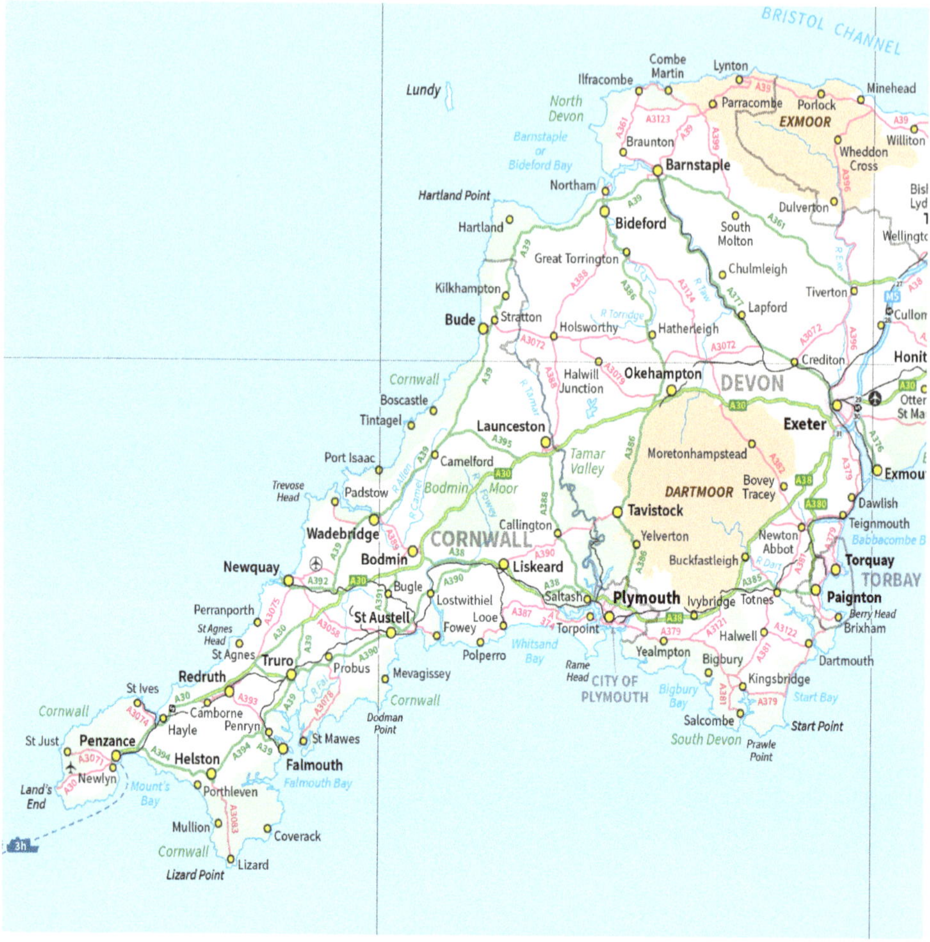

The South West of England

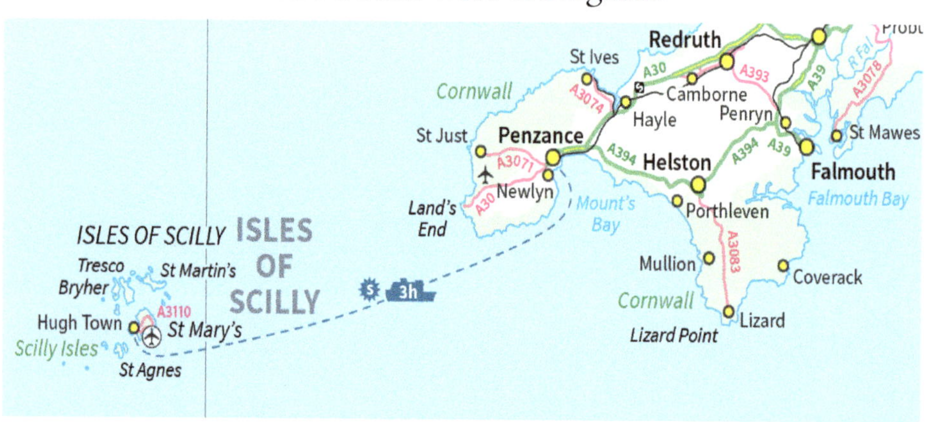

West Cornwall

Contents

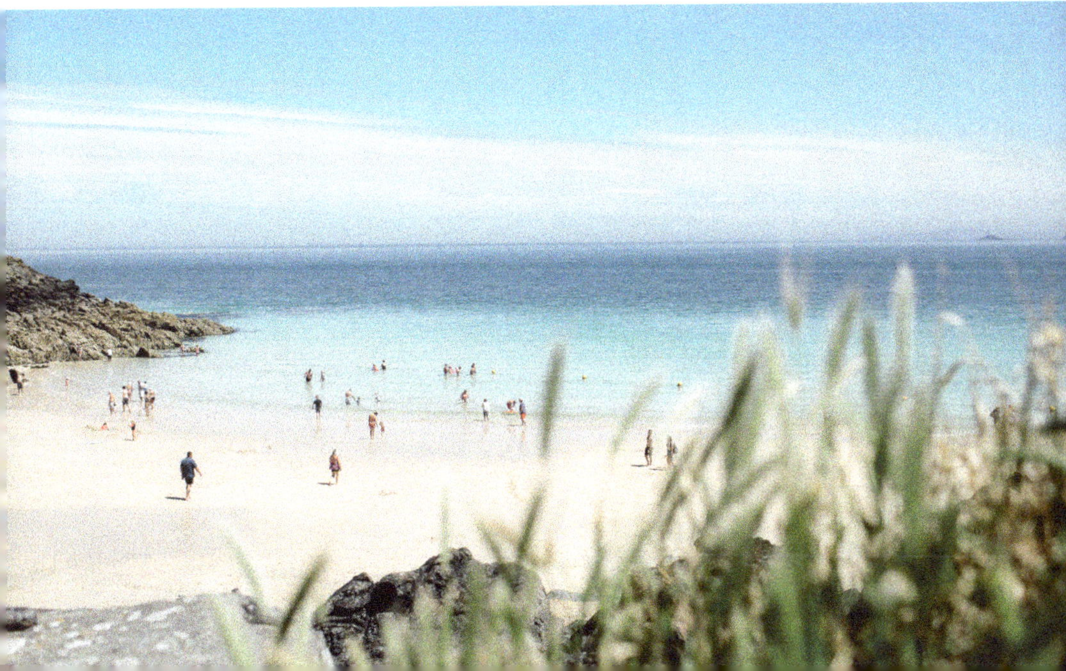

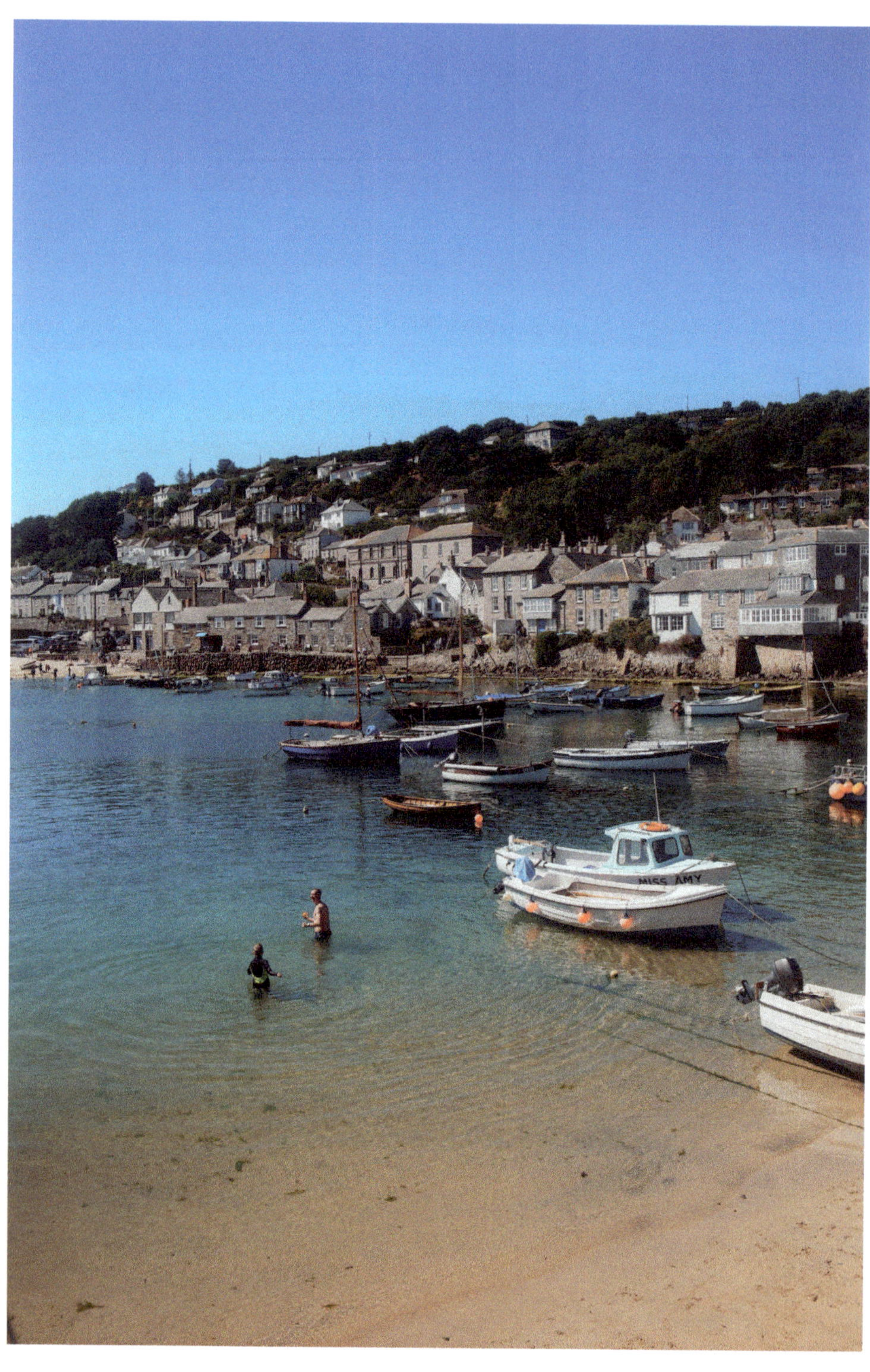
MISS AMY

Introduction

The stunning coastline of Cornwall is surrounded by mystery, legend and sheer beauty. The tales of pirates and smugglers really come to life when you get out and spend some time walking the fabulous coast path of this breath taking county, especially when speaking to the locals in the numerous little harbours and picturesque villages.

In some ways West Cornwall feels even more remote, and sometimes you can walk all day along the coast without seeing another soul. At times like this, when at the mercy of the elements, you can really appreciate the power and energy of the land and sea, which combine to invigorate and really give you a sense of mystery and wonder.

It is true to say that West Cornwall is unique and the coastline is absolutely stunning. You can often be left speechless when confronted with the sights, sounds and smells which wash over your senses when on this remote peninsula.

From the little fishing villages and harbours you will walk into larger settlements like St Ives, which has to be one of the prettiest small towns in the British Isles, with its beautiful beaches, amazingly relaxed atmosphere and mouth-watering restaurants.

I have spent a lot of time in West Cornwall, and during this time I have walked around its coastal path several times. I will never tire of its beauty, and the feelings which are invoked within me when in this most beautiful part of England are rarely replicated anywhere else. I am not alone when talking about my feelings for this area, as there are many who, like me, are also enchanted by and have fallen completely in love with this part of Cornwall. If given the chance, I could literally spend my whole lifetime rambling around this stunning coastline.

In this book I would like to present to you some of the pleasure that I have had, whilst spending time in West Cornwall. If you are not able, or lucky enough to be able to get out on the West Cornwall coast path, then I really hope that the photographs in this book will help you to enjoy some of its unique coastal scenery. It is my wish that after seeing these images, it will inspire you to get out and have your own adventures along Cornwall's lovely sea-swept coastline. If you do, I am certain that you will also find it hard not to fall in love with, and become completely enchanted by its intoxicating atmosphere.

Portreath to Godrevy Point

This is a fabulous stretch of coastline, which will give you a taste of what's to come as you make your way around West Cornwall. From the golden sand and surfing at Portreath, the coast weaves it's way past the impressive Gull Rock, the awe-inspiring landscape at Ralph's Cupboard, the beauty of Hell's Mouth, and finally the icing on the cake as Godrevy Lighthouse comes in to view.

There is something for everyone on this little stretch of Cornwall's amazing coast, including a secluded beach at Mutton Cove where seals can often be seen with their pups, whilst stretched out on the sand and soaking up the Cornish sunshine.

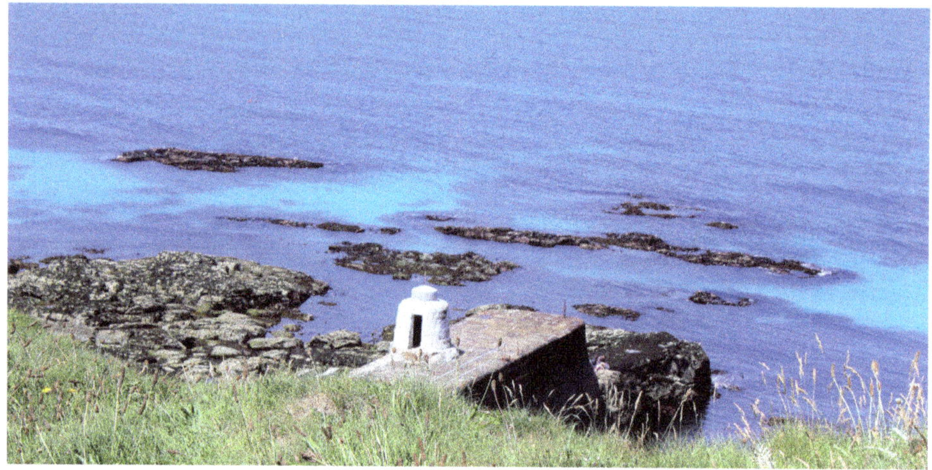

The Lighthouse, or 'monkey hut' at Portreath Harbour.

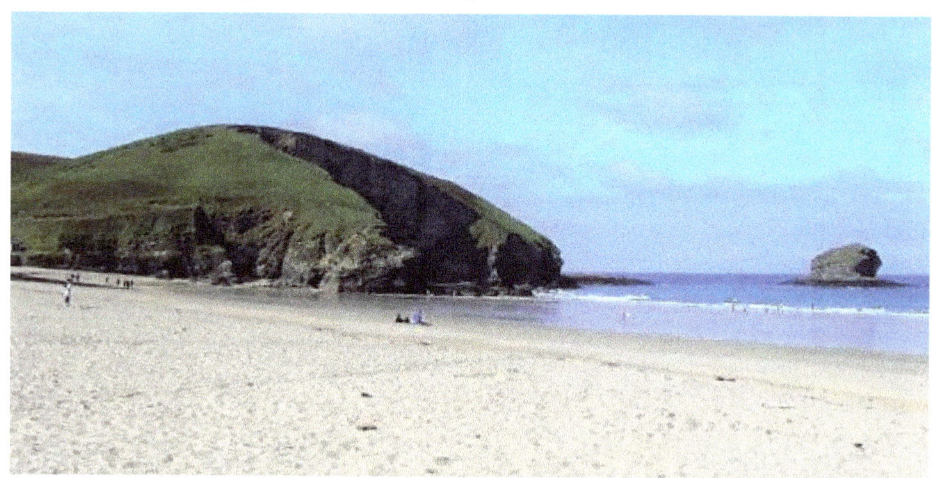

Looking across Portreath beach, with Gull Rock out in the ocean.

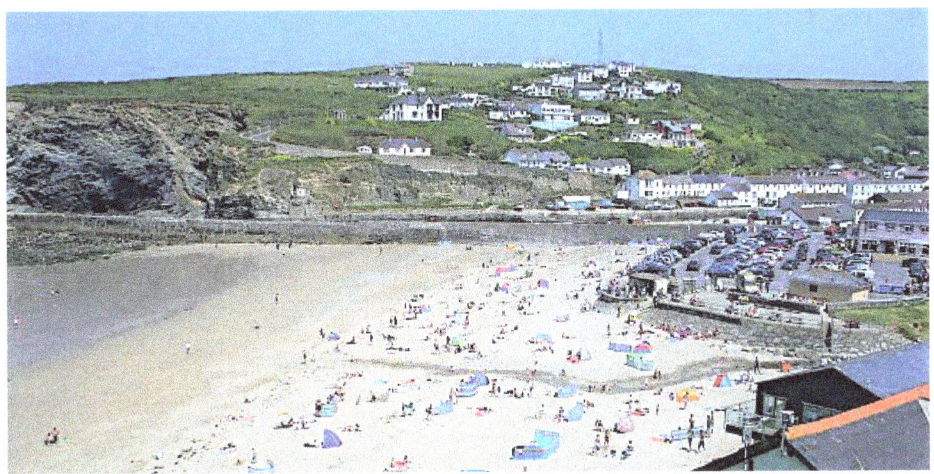
The view across Portreath beach, to its village nestling into the hill behind.

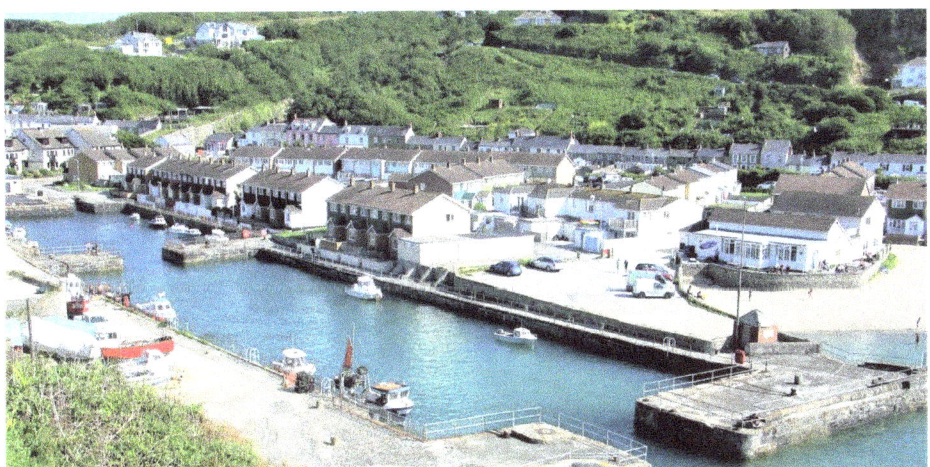
Portreath's compact harbour is at the heart of the village.

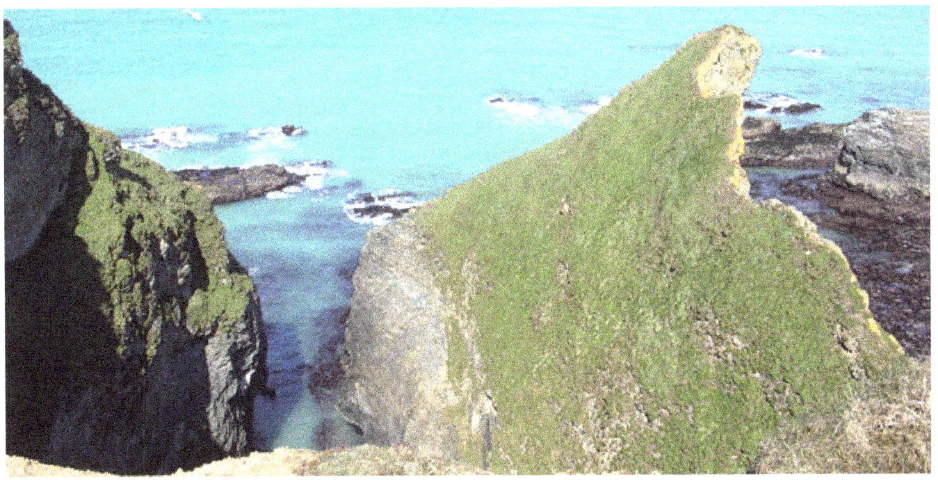
After leaving Portreath, you will see the stunning Ralph's Cupboard.

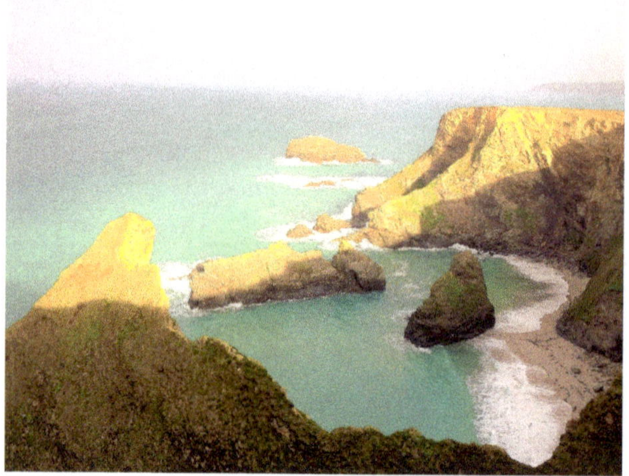

Looking north towards Ralph's Cupboard.

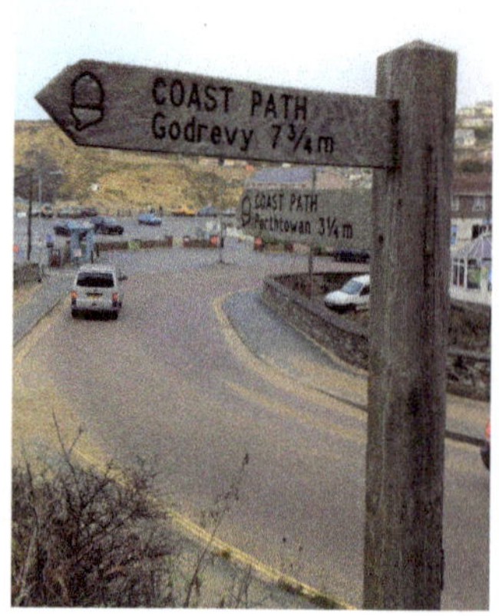

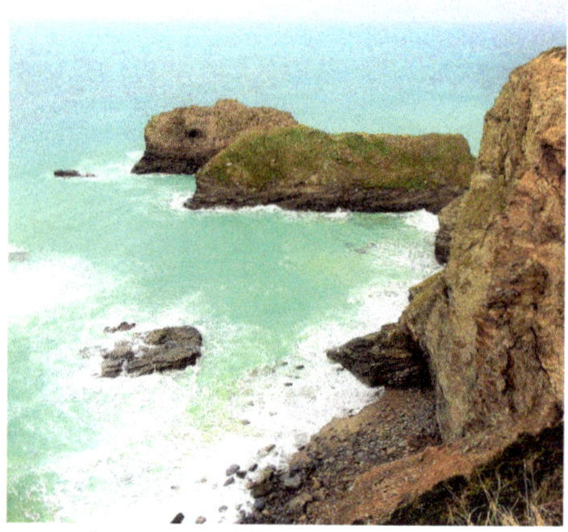

The Beautiful Samphire Island.

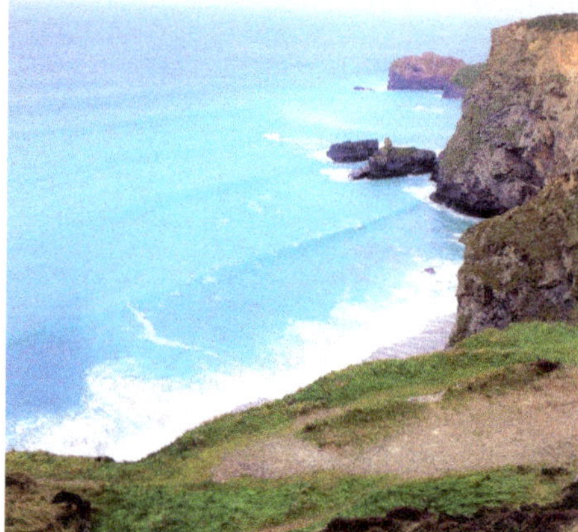

The surf crashing into a secluded bay.

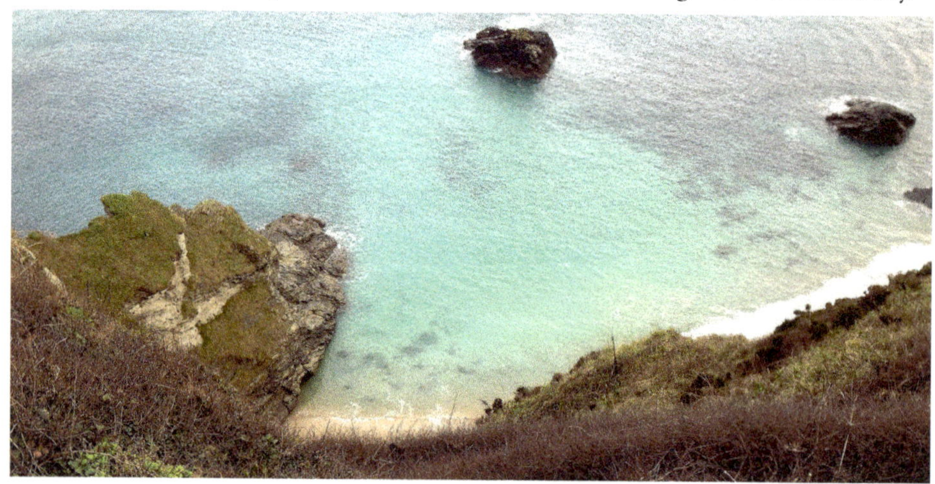

Glimpses of beautiful turquoise sea.

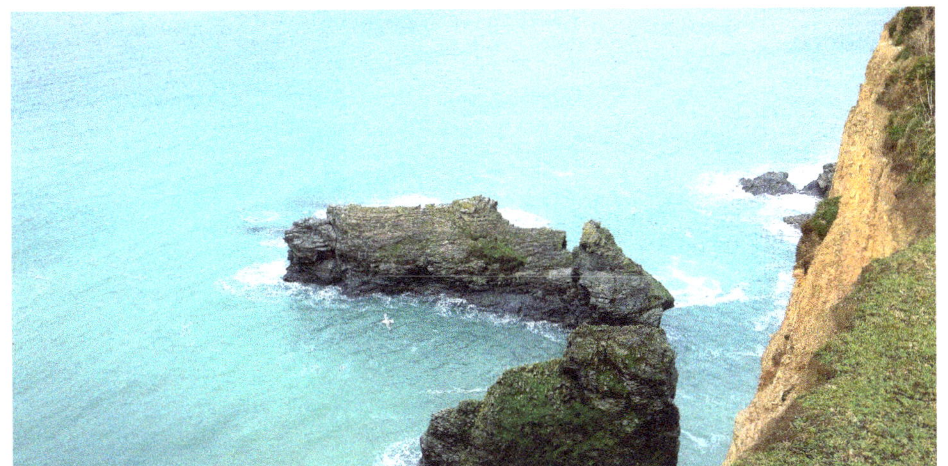

The view along this section of path is simply breathtaking.

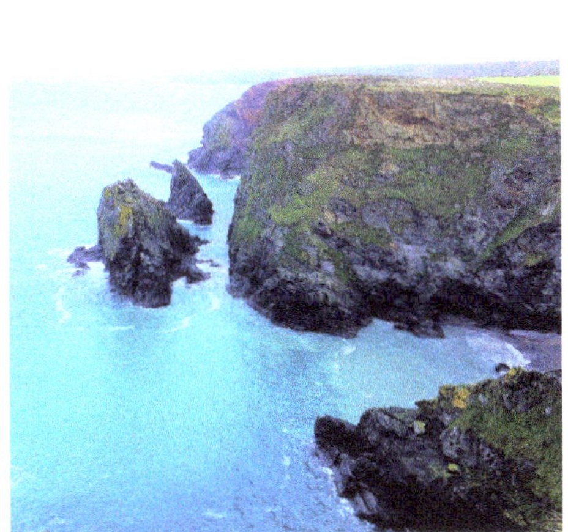

The stunning Hell's Mouth.

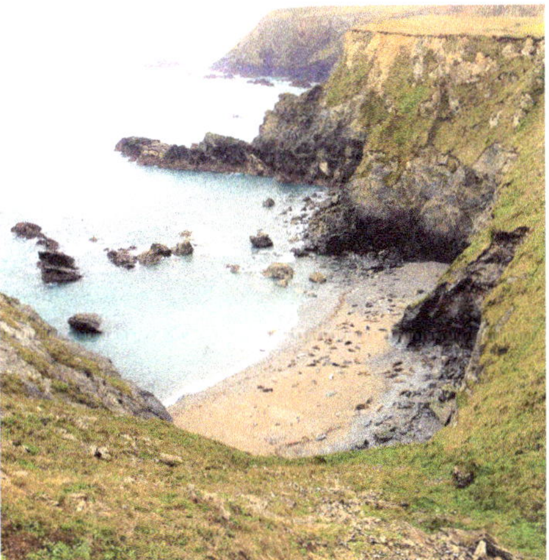

Seals on the beach at Mutton Cove.

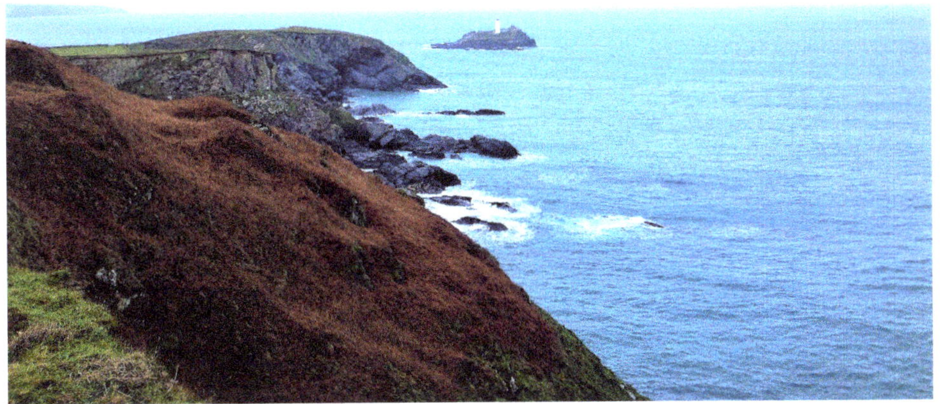

Nearing the Hayle Towans (Cornish for dunes), with views of Godrevy Lighthouse.

When standing at Godrevy Point and looking out to sea, you will be rewarded with the majestic view of Godrevy Lighthouse. This strong lighthouse has been warning ships and fishing vessels of the surrounding stone reefs since 1859. It is a really wonderful sight that can be seen from miles around as it towers (approx. 26m tall) above Godrevy Island.

The lighthouse and surrounding area was also the inspiration for Virginia Woolf's famous novel 'To the Lighthouse', which she penned back in 1927 after spending time in the area.

Stretching between Godrevy and the town of Hayle is the fabulous Hayle Beaches with their large 'towans' (Cornish for sand dunes). Here you will find 3 miles of golden sand with beautiful blue sea behind it. Looking out across the sea, you will also be able to see the pretty towns of Lelant and Carbis, with the glorious town of St Ives in the distance.

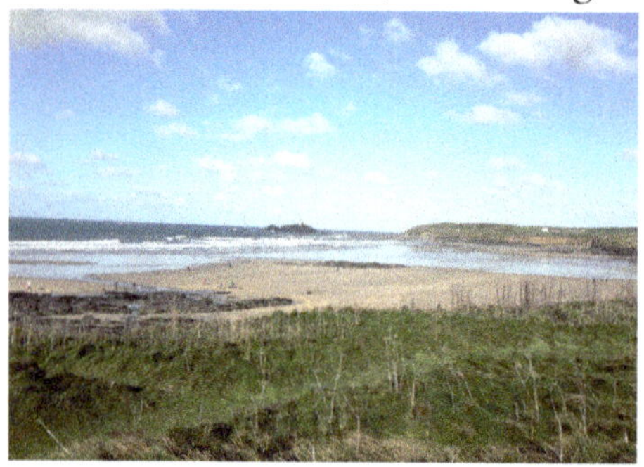

Looking north towards Godrevy Point.

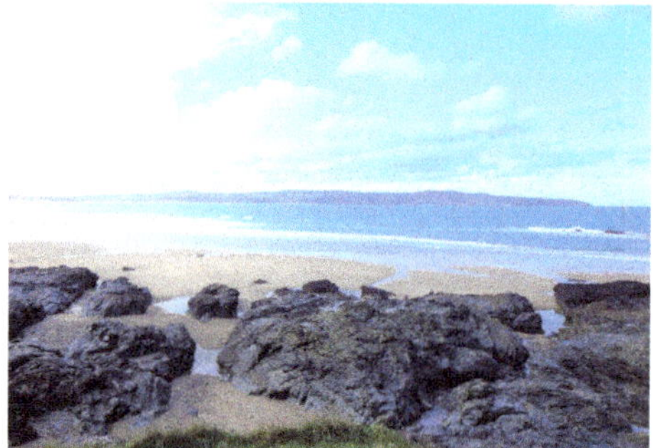

At the north end of Hayle Beaches.

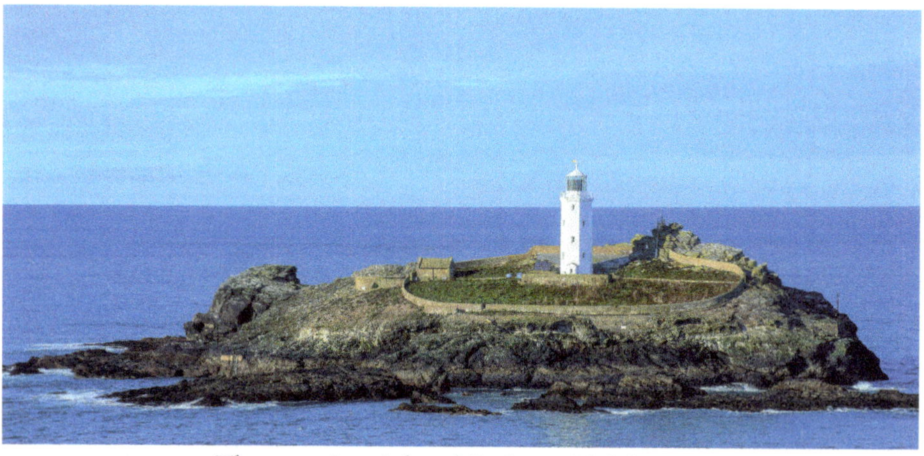

The stunning sight of Godrevy Lighthouse.

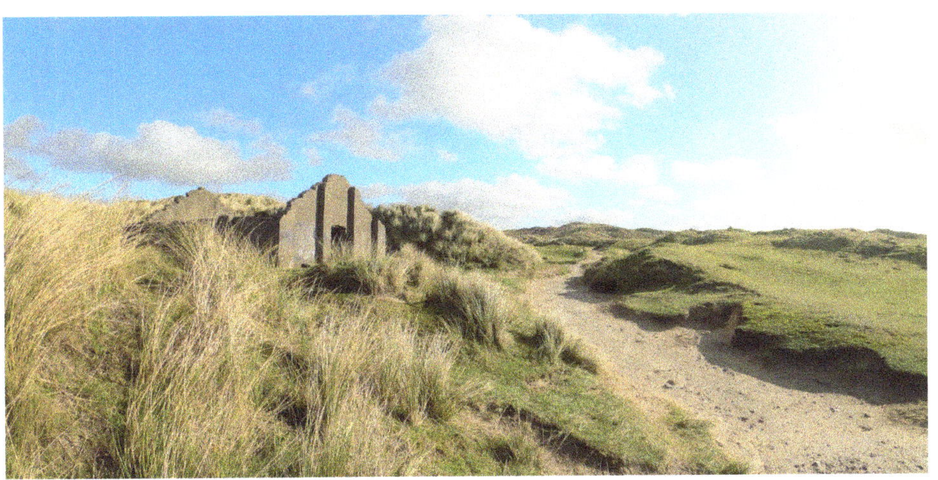

Peace and solitude can always be found in 'The Towans' .

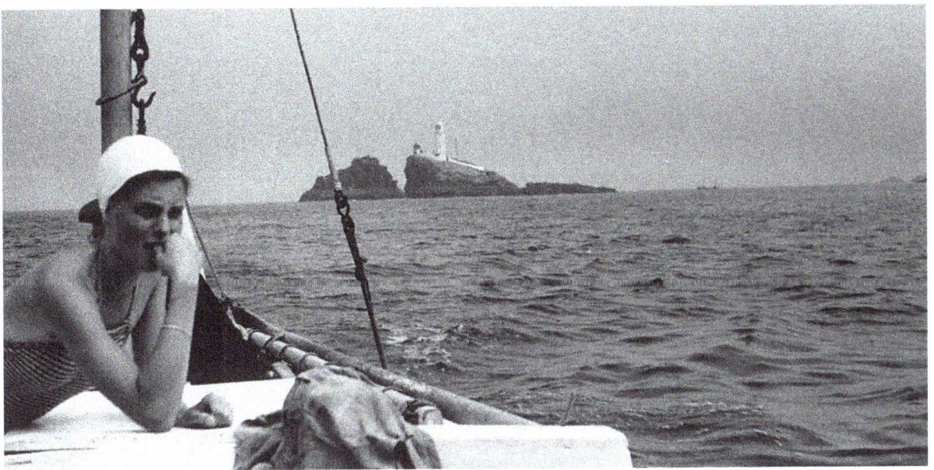

On a boat trip to Godrevy Lighthouse. Taken in 1949.

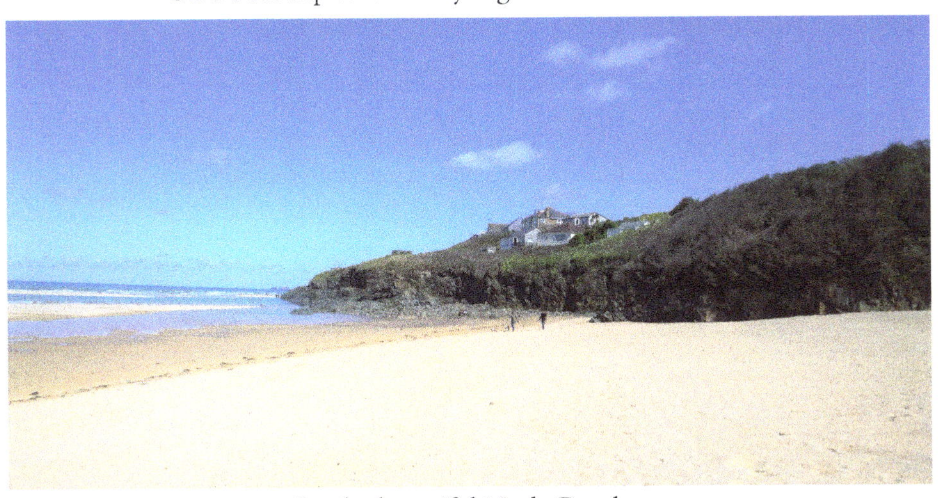

On the beautiful Hayle Beaches.

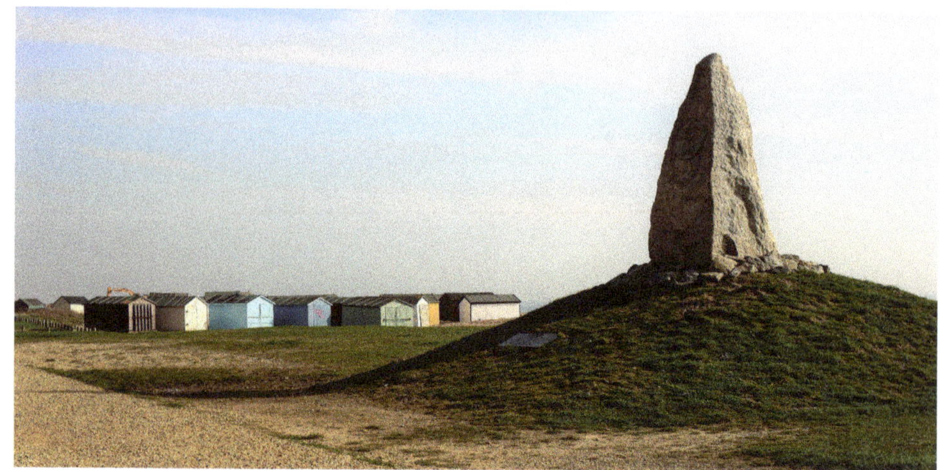
A standing stone monument, in The Towans.

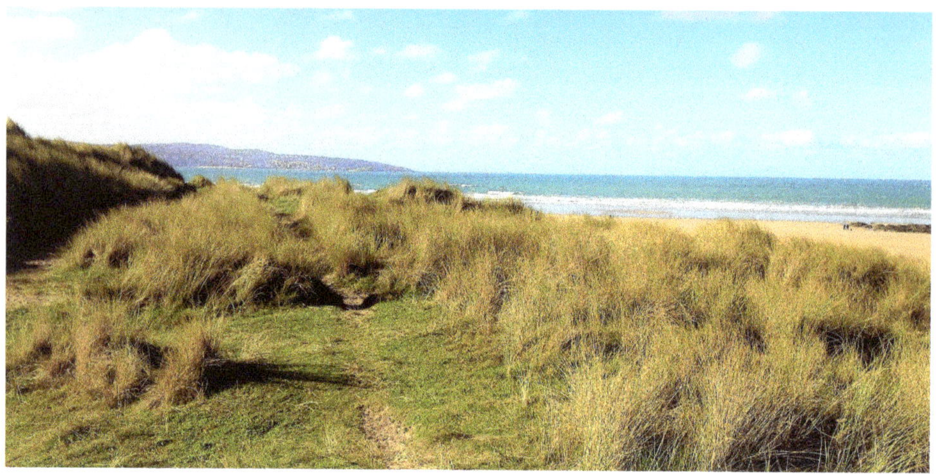
Waking through Hayle Towans (sand dunes).

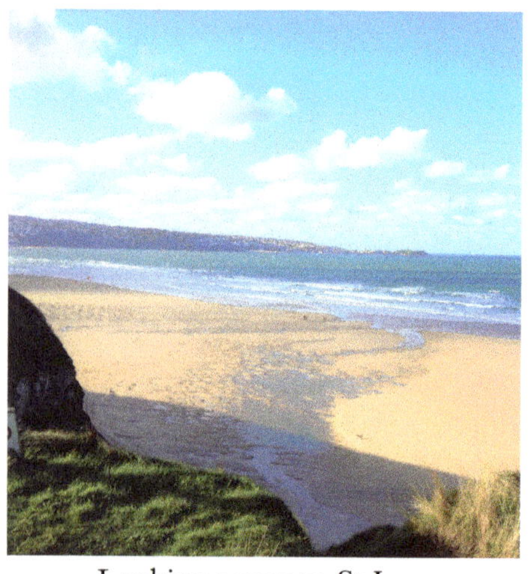
Looking across to St Ives.

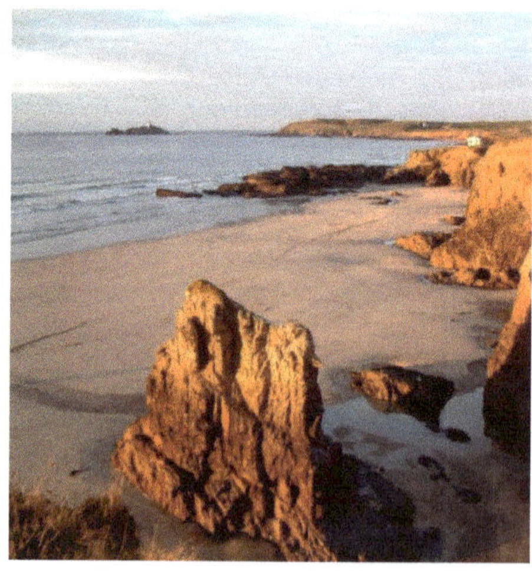
A sunset on Hayle Beaches.

Hayle to St Ives

Upon leaving the town of Hayle and crossing its estuary, the pretty little village of Lelant will soon appear. Here you will be able to see the coastal church of St Uny's and the lovely Porth Kidney Sands.

Around the headland of Carrack Gladden, Porth Kidney Sands merges with Carbis Bay which has a pretty beach of golden sand. Just above the beach is the well-known Carbis Bay Hotel, with the village sitting just behind. This is a popular holiday destination for those seeking some peace and quiet next to the bays deep blue sea, with lots of invigorating fresh air.

Just around the next headland of Porthminster Point is the breathtaking town of St Ives. St Ives is just stunning, with its beautiful golden beaches being complemented by the translucent, and often turquoise sea which completely surrounds the town.

St Ives is one of Cornwall's true gems, which has something for everyone. Excellent food, history, art, fresh air and sheer beauty are merged into an unforgettable experience. There is surfing at Porthmeor beach, to relaxing and sun-worshipping at the pretty beaches of Bamaluz, Porthgwidden and Porthminster. The harbourside is delightful where you can always watch fishing boats coming and going, and you will often see the odd seal, and sometimes even dolphins if you are lucky enough.

The art scene has blossomed in St Ives over the past century, with many famous artists flocking there to make use of the incredibly clear light and beautiful scenery for their paintings. Noted artists that have lived in St Ives include the locally born Alfred Wallis (1855-1942), and the world renowned sculptor and artist Barbara Hepworth. At the bottom of Barnoon Hill you can visit the house which Barbara used to work and live in, which has been turned into a museum in her memory.

Art is so popular in St Ives that the Tate Gallery of London built the 'Tate St Ives' which overlooks the beautiful Porthmeor Beach.

St Ives was built up around the fishing industry, which has been in operation in the town since the Middle Ages. This peaked during the 19th century with the worldwide demand for locally caught pilchards.

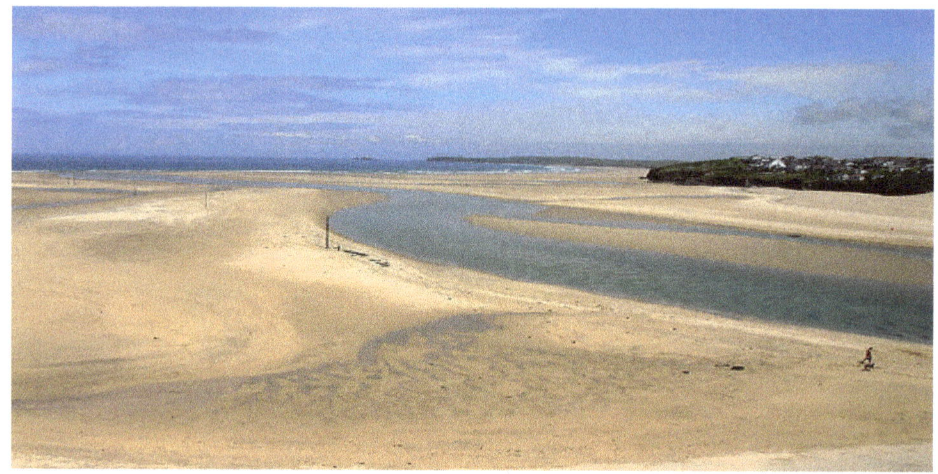

The view across the Hayle Estuary from Porth Kidney Sands.

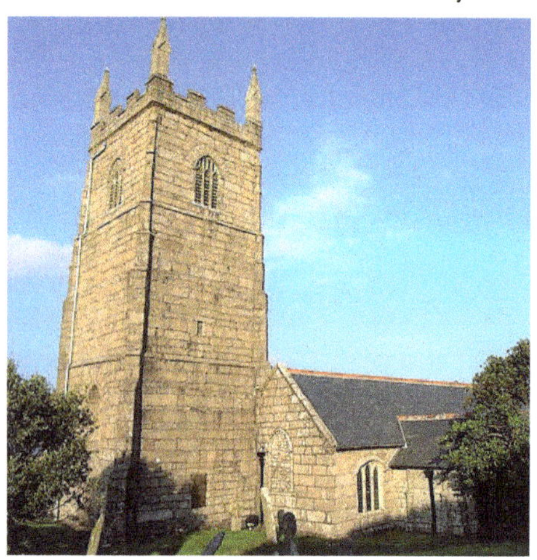

The church of St Uny's, Lelant.

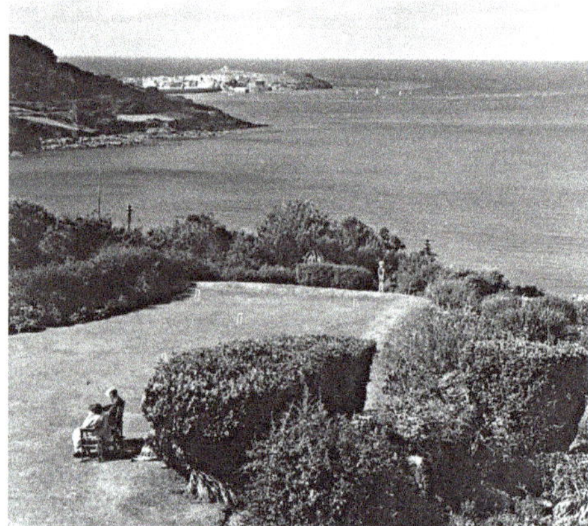

Carbis Hotel (1940's), St Ives behind.

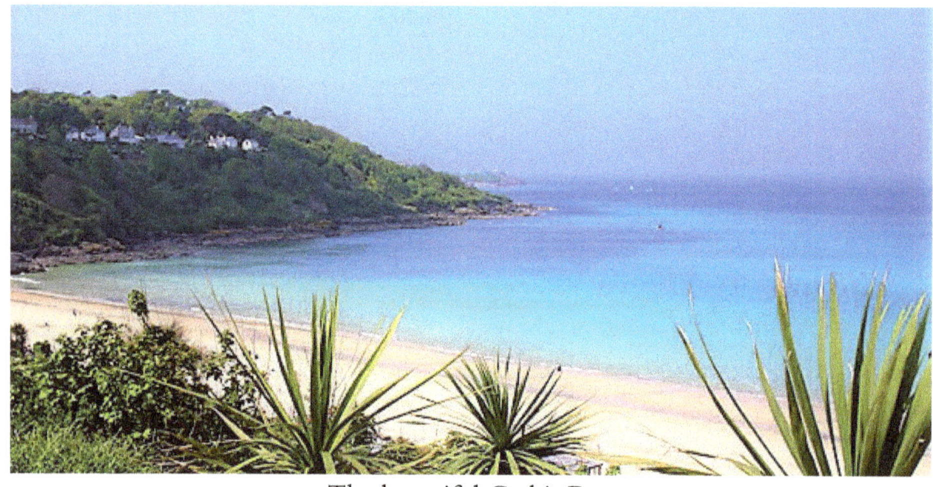

The beautiful Carbis Bay.

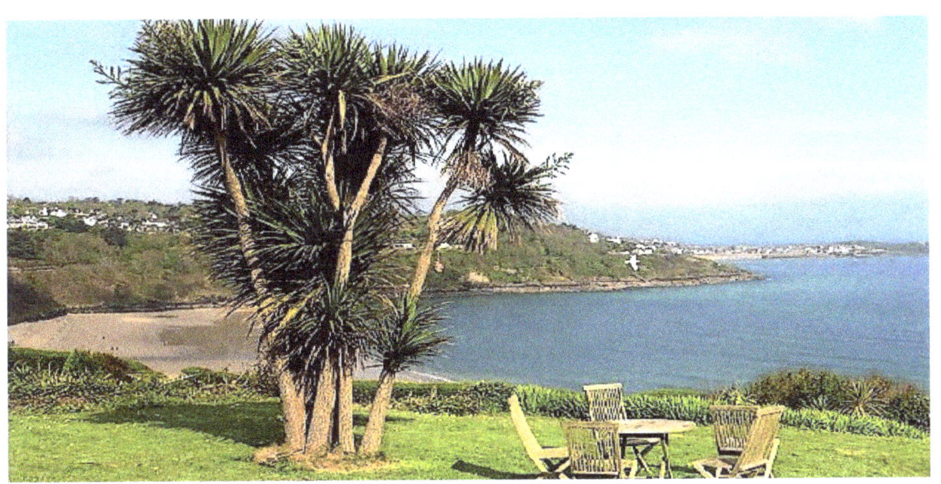

Overlooking Carbis Bay with a glimpse of St Ives on the far right.

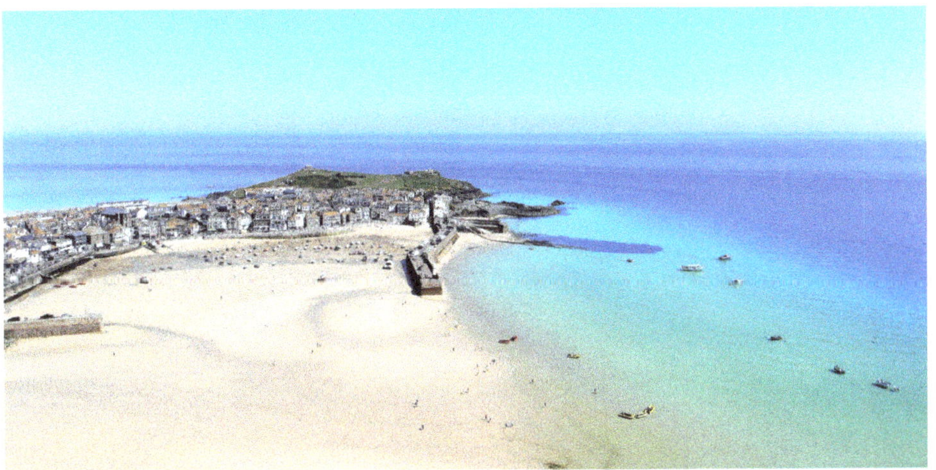

The astounding beauty of St Ives.

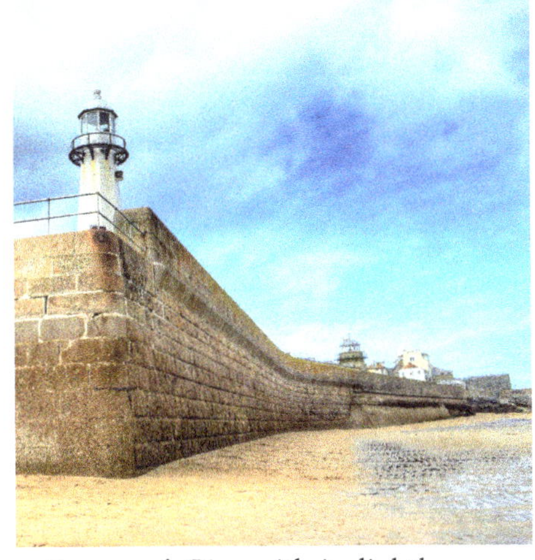

Smeaton's Pier with its lighthouse.

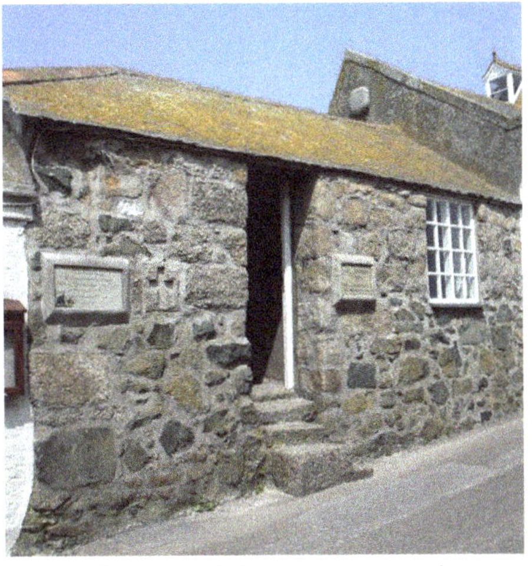

The Old fisherman's chapel.

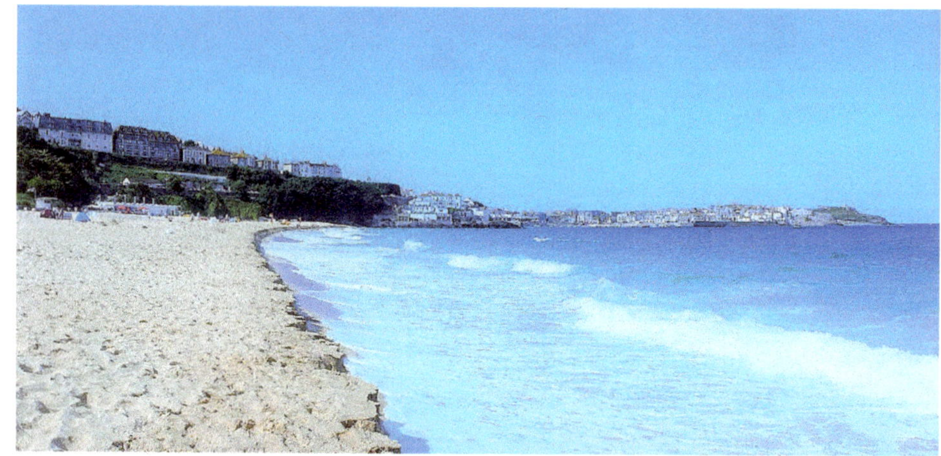

On the beautiful Porthminster Beach, St Ives.

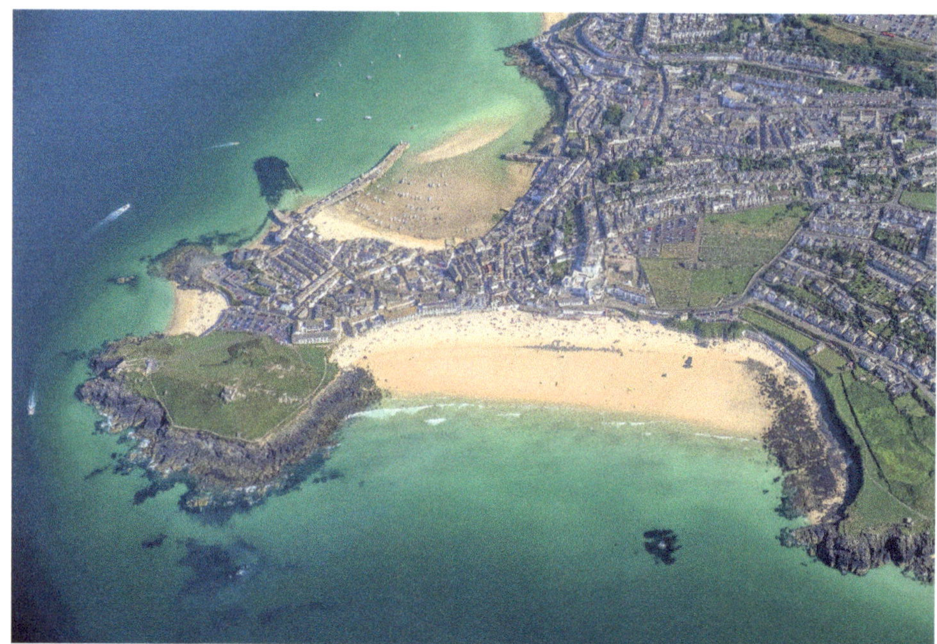

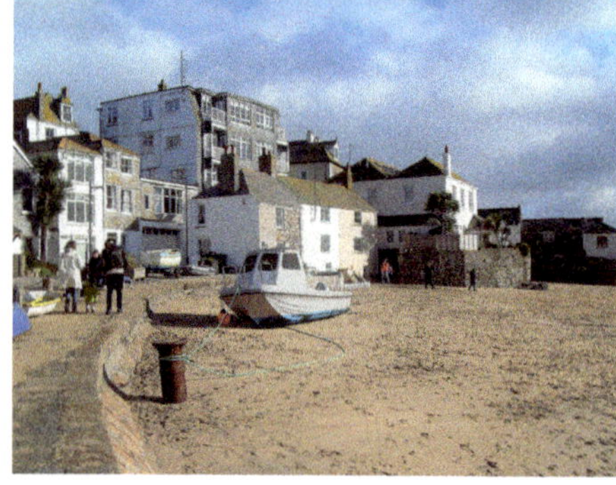

Fishermen's cottages at The Harbour.

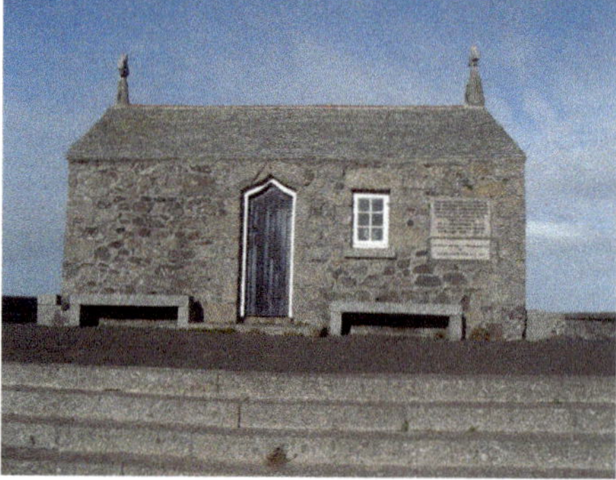

St Nicholas Chapel on 'The Island.'

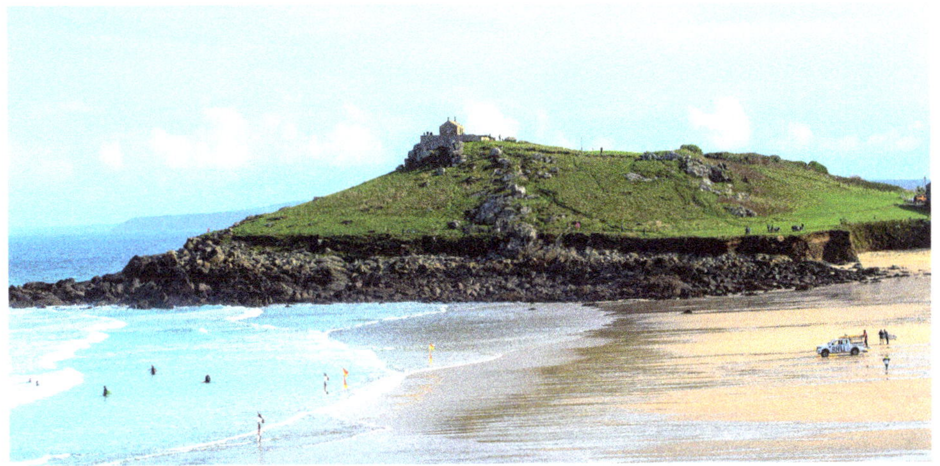

Looking across the beautiful Porthmeor Beach to St Ives Head (The Island).

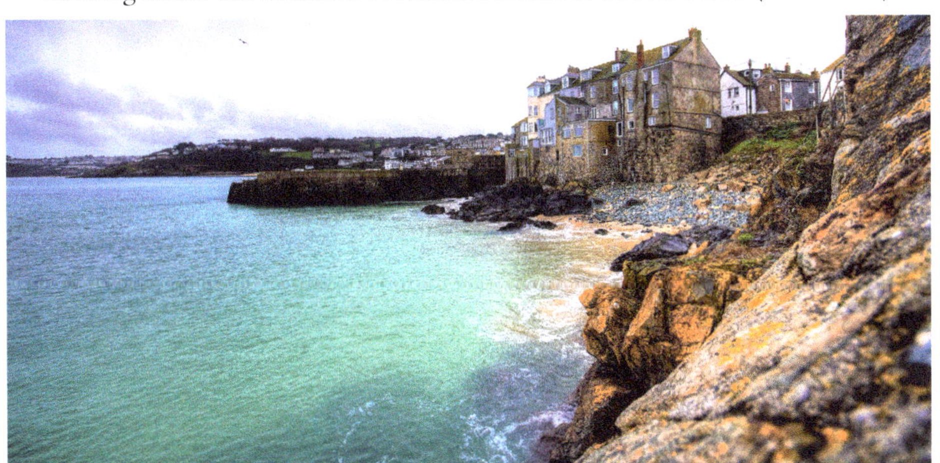

A stormy day at Bamaluz Beach.

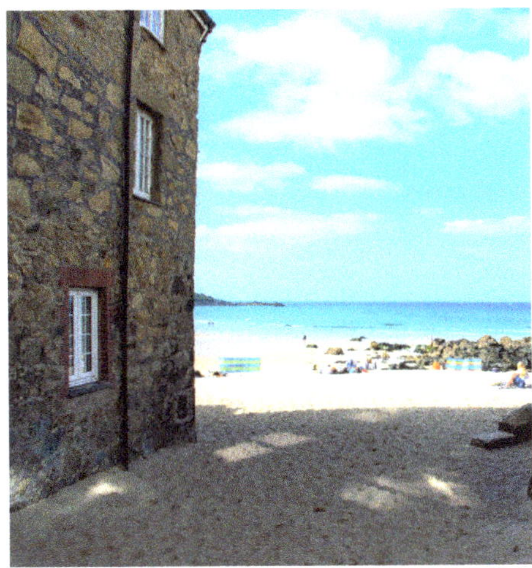

At the east end of Porthmeor Beach.

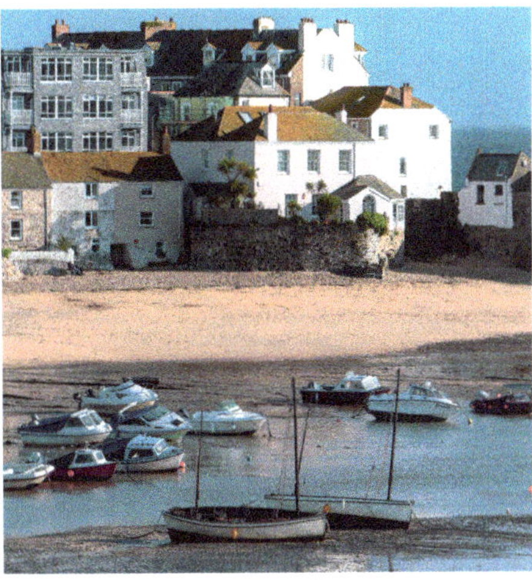

St Ives Harbour.

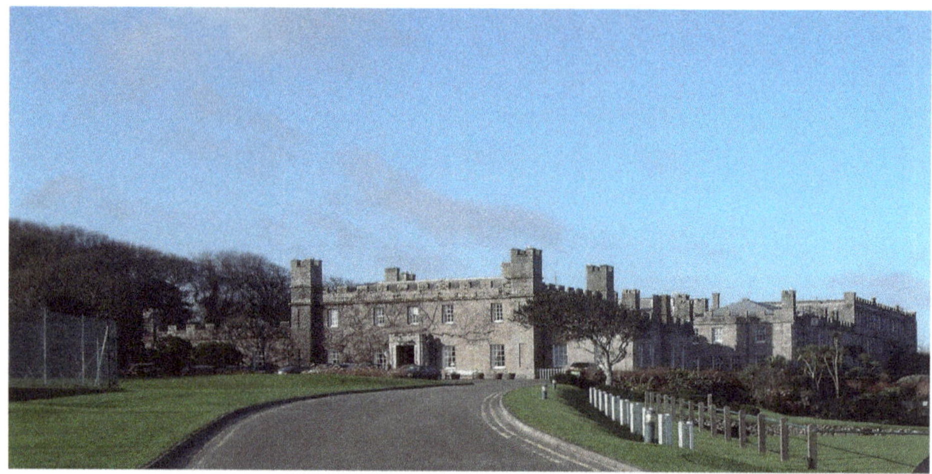

The front entrance to Tregenna Castle Estate which sits on the hill above St Ives.

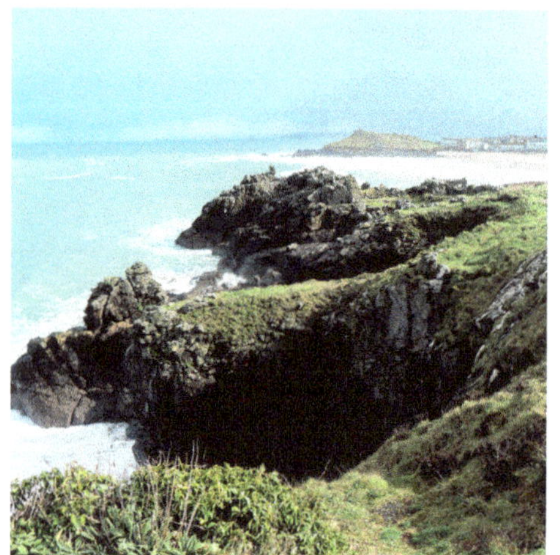

Carrick Du headland, west St Ives.

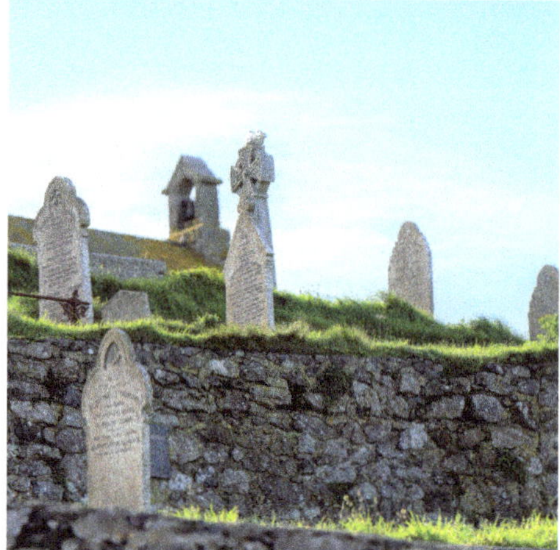

Barnoon cemetery.

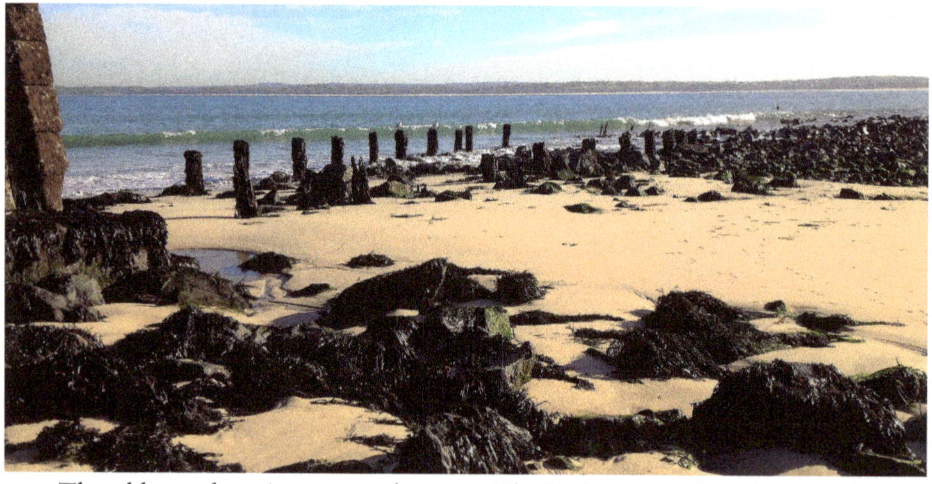

The old wooden pier stumps, between The Habour and Bamaluz Beach.

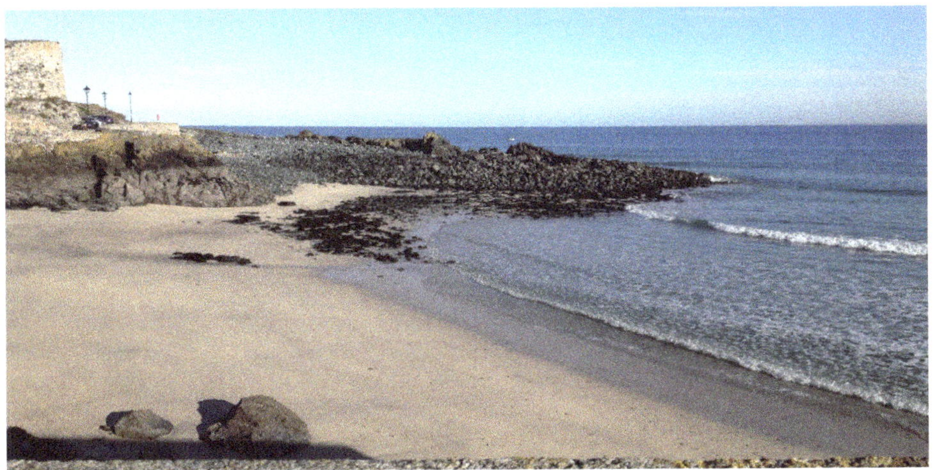

The wonderful Bamaluz Beach from the south.

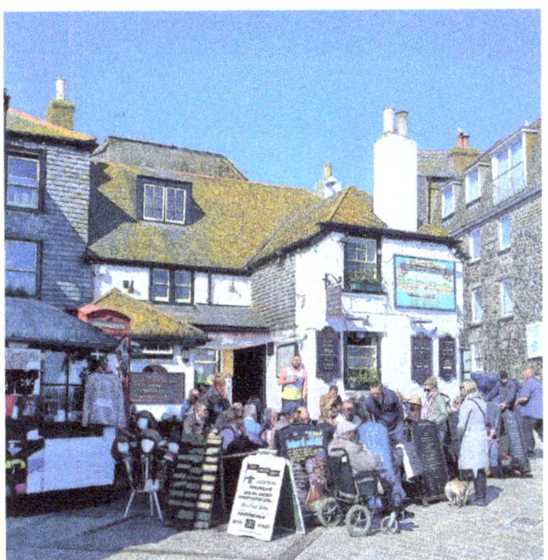

The ancient pub, The Sloop.

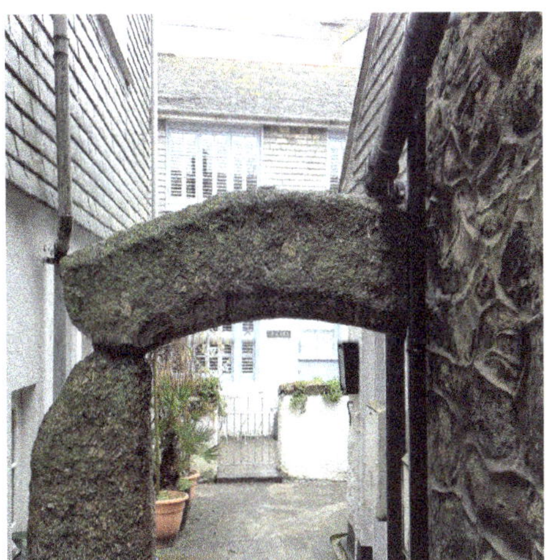

The Old Arch near The Digey.

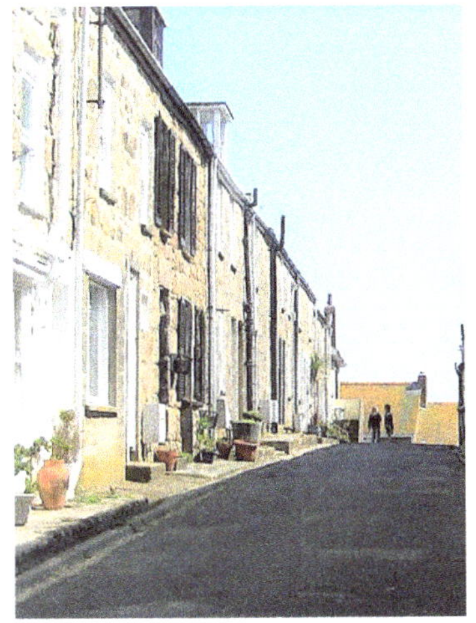

The old streets in Downalong.

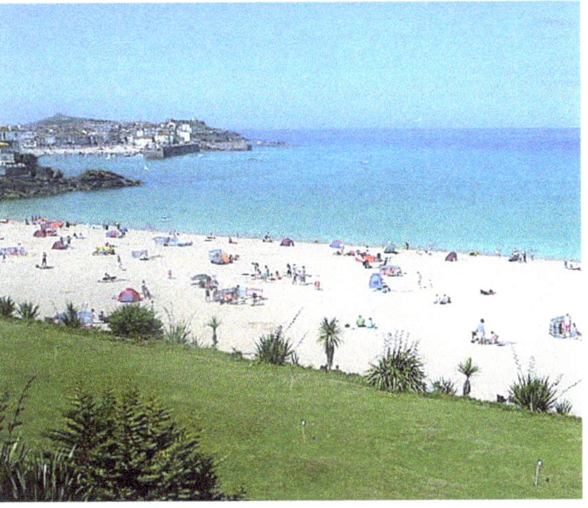

Enjoying the sea and sun, at Porthminster Beach.

St Ives to Zennor

The coastline after St Ives becomes more remote, which makes for some of the best coastal walking in the county. It is often said that the coast between St Ives and the rest of West Cornwall is the most remote on the south west coast path, and will afford you with some outstanding coastal scenery.

From jagged, rocky headlands to secluded little coves and beaches, this next section will give you everything. On a still day the water will be lapping up to the shore with sparkling deep blues and turquoise.

But during stormy days this section can have quite an ominous feel to it, where you can really sense that you are at the mercy of the elements and the power of nature can really be felt in every sense.

About 200 metres off shore is a small group of islands called The Carracks. The largest of which is often called Seal Island by the locals as it is home to many Atlantic grey seals.

Along the coast nearer to St Ives can be found 'the merry harvesters' which is a recently constructed stone circle, which has fooled many a traveller into thinking that they are very ancient, much to the merriment of the locals.

As the coastline nears Zennor, the impressive Wicca Pool comes into view which is a fairly large bay. The word wicca comes from Anglo-Saxon and was a term used to denote a wise person or sorcerer, and in more modern times a branch of witchcraft was given this name by its founder Gerald Gardener. So perhaps the area got its name from the 'wicca' that may have lived in these parts many centuries ago.

Columns of granite will add to the beauty of the coastline all around West Cornwall from St Ives onwards, which really add to its beauty and ruggedness, and it gives the Cornish coastline a totally unique look.

At Zennor Head you will also get glimpses of the impressive promontory of Gurnard's Head, which is on the next section of coastline. Inland from here is the remote little village of Zennor, where its old pub 'The Tinners Arms' makes for a fantastic place to stop and get some good food and ale. It also has an ancient church which contains a carved seat, depicting the ancient legend of 'the mermaid of Zennor'.

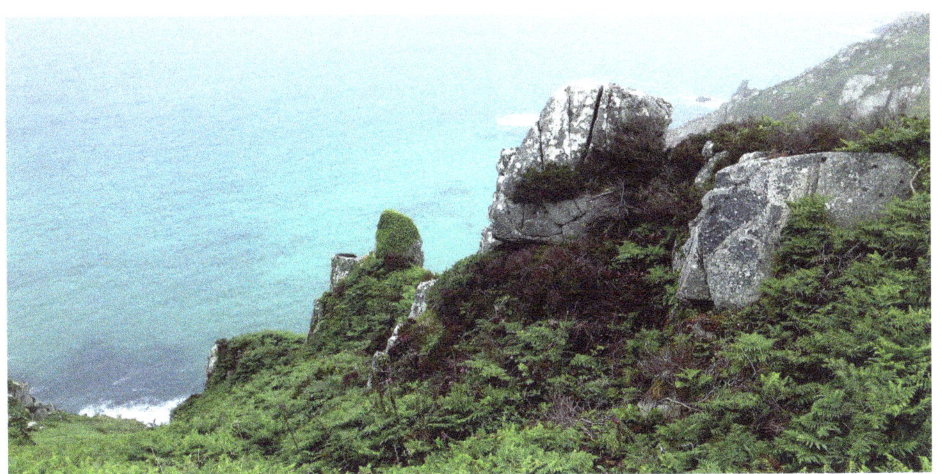

Blue sea and granite rock formations.

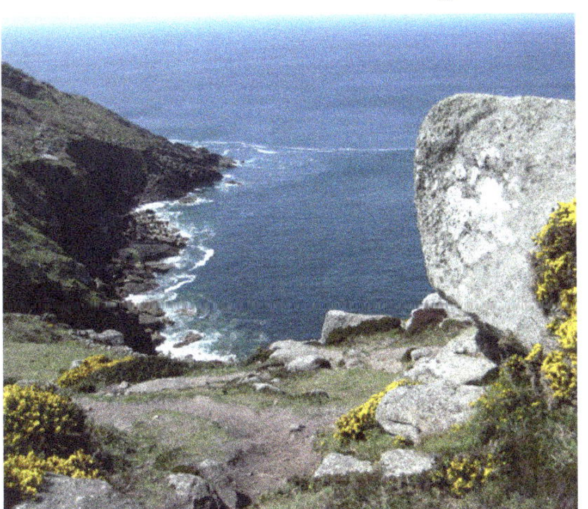

Remote rocky headlands.

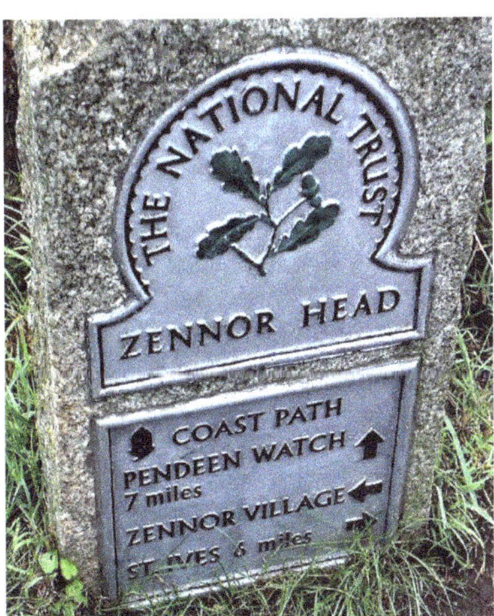

En-route to Zennor Head.

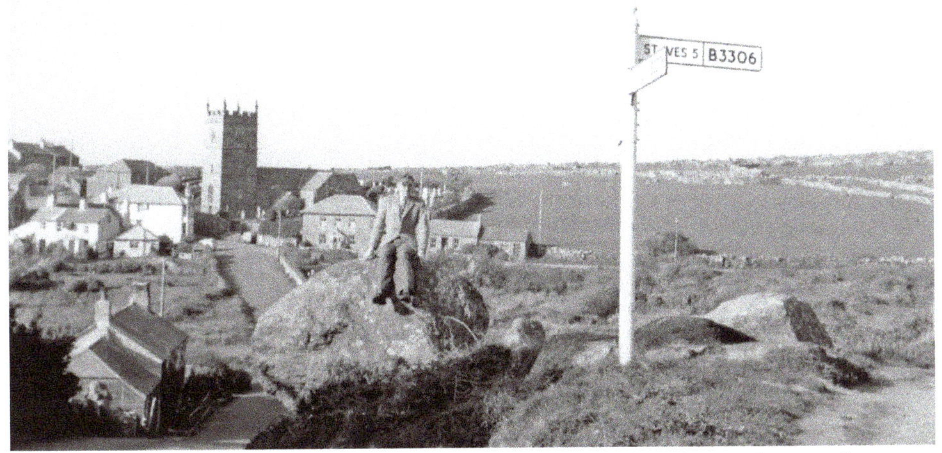

Zennor in the mid 20th century, virtually nothing has changed since then.

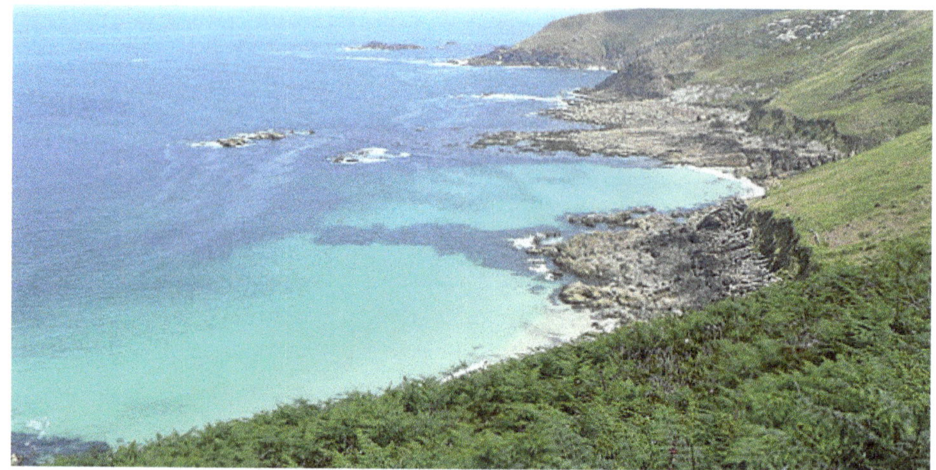

The coast path on a sunny day, with turquoise water.

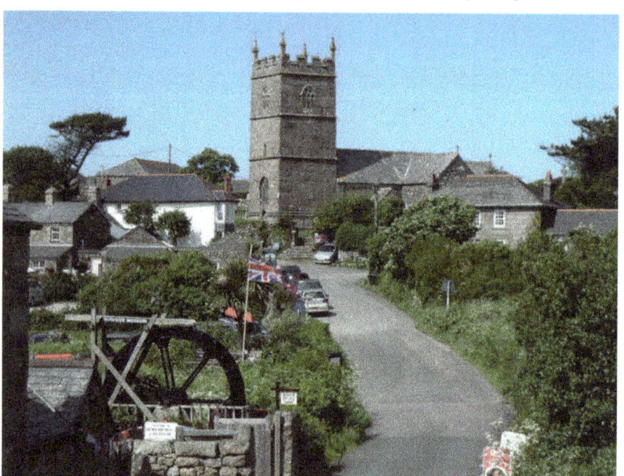

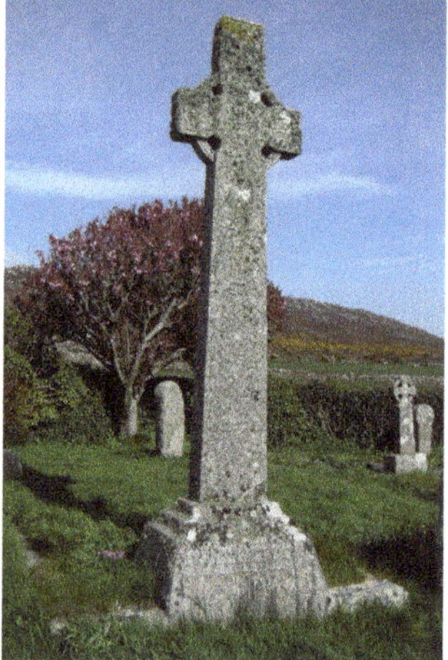

Zennor church where the mermaid seat is kept. A Cornish cross in the graveyard.

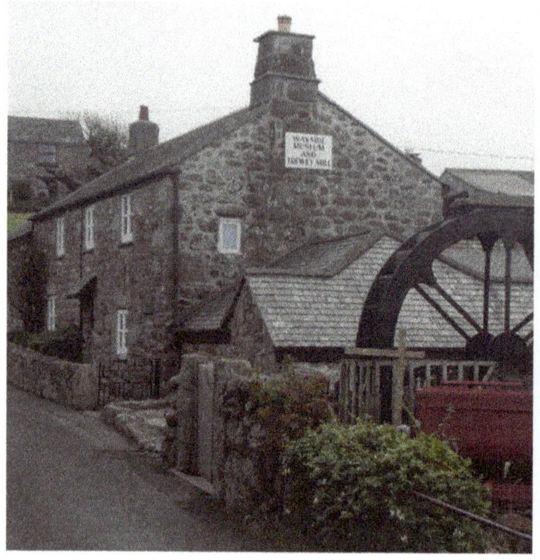

The Old Mill.

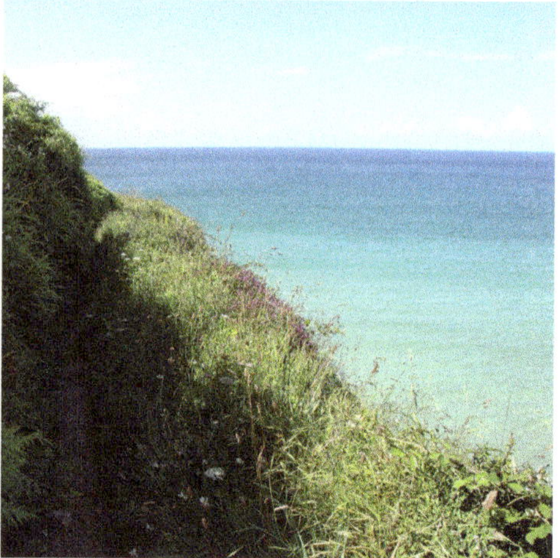

The beautiful coastal path.

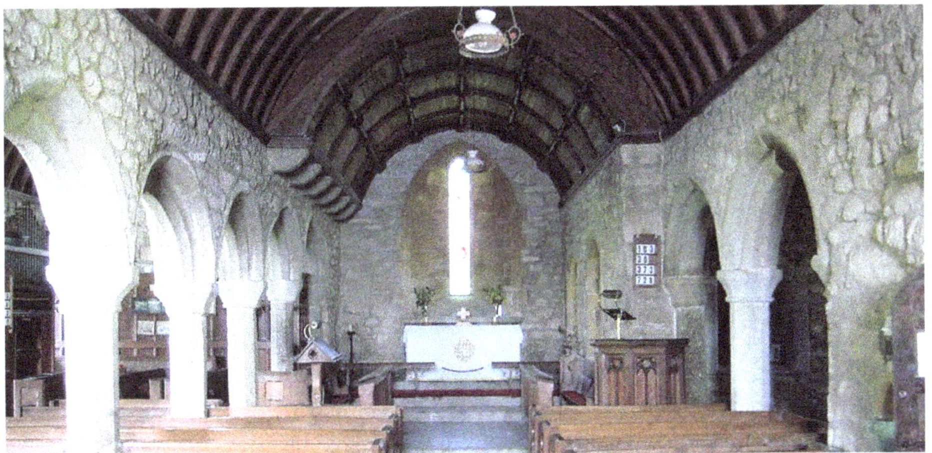

Inside Zennor's church, which is dedicated to St Senara.

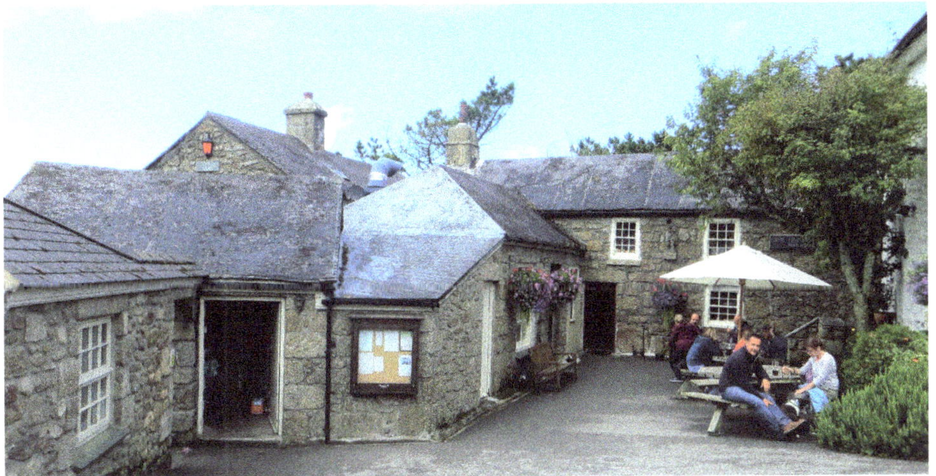

The Tinners Arms which dates back to 1271AD.

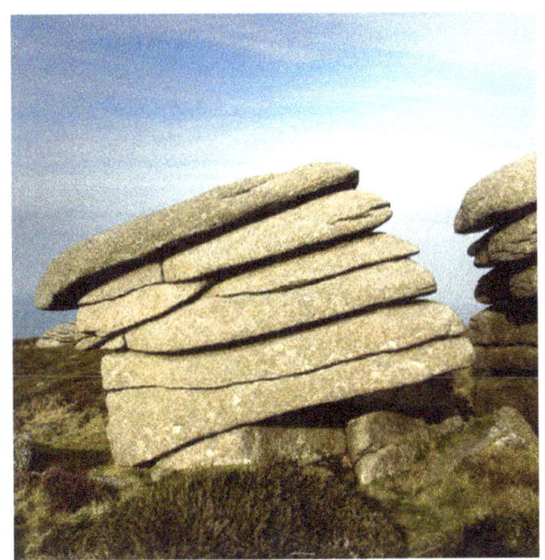

Granite rock formations.

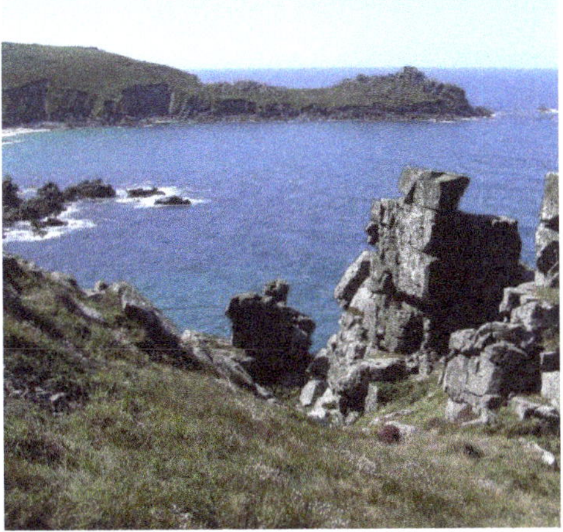

Looking towards Gurnard's Head.

Zennor to Pendeen Watch

After leaving Zennor the coastline remains very remote, and with its rugged beauty this really is a stunning section of West Cornwall.

The first headland which is passed after Zennor, is the breath-taking promontory of Gurnard's Head. This is a truly iconic part of the coast path which juts out into the Atlantic ocean like a large sleeping whale.

Towards the end of this section the wonderful sight of Pendeen Watch Lighthouse will come into view. The tower stands at 17metres and was designed by the engineer Sir Thomas Matthews back in 1891. Within the buildings at Pendeen Watch is also a large foghorn to warn any ships of the impending danger during times of poor visibility.

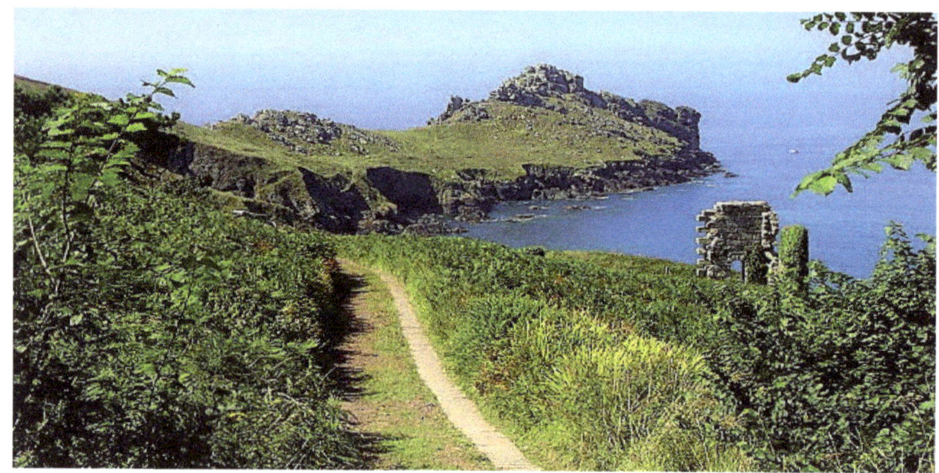

Approaching Gurnard's Head after leaving Zennor Head.

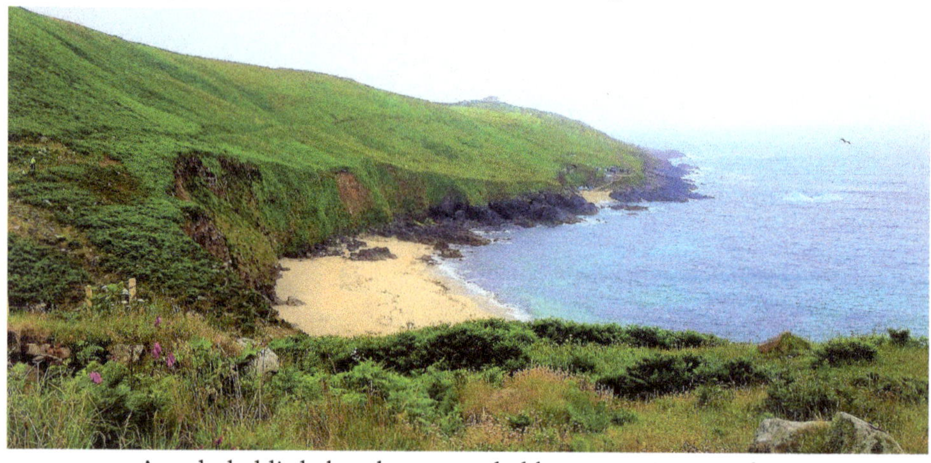

A secluded little beach surrounded by a stunning coastline.

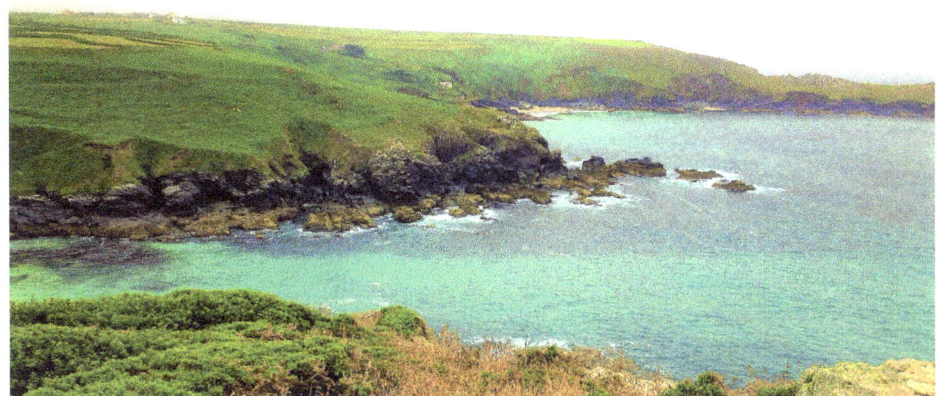

Porthglaze Cove which is just to the west of Zennor.

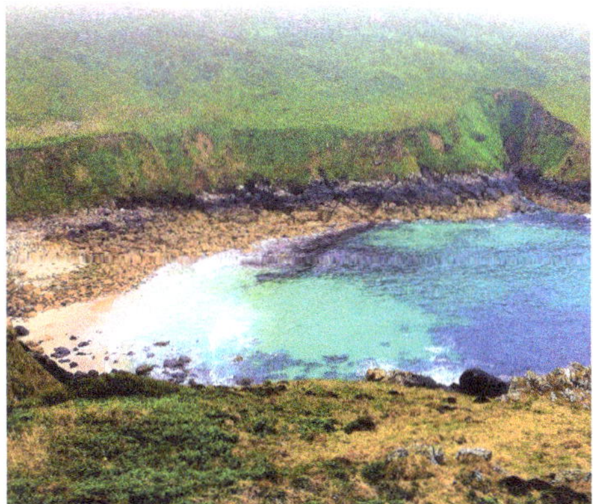

Remote rocky headlands.

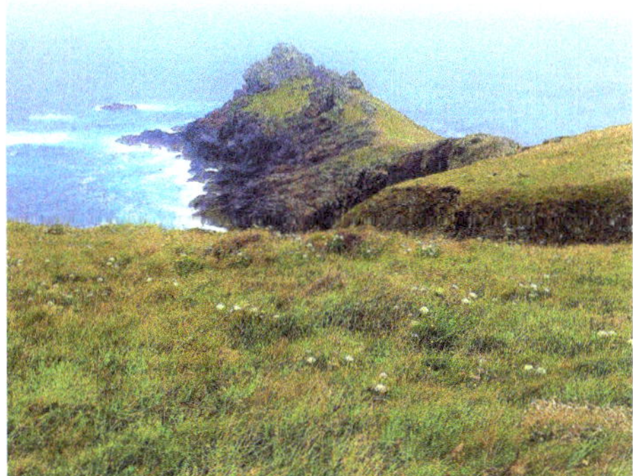

Looking out at Gurnard's Head.

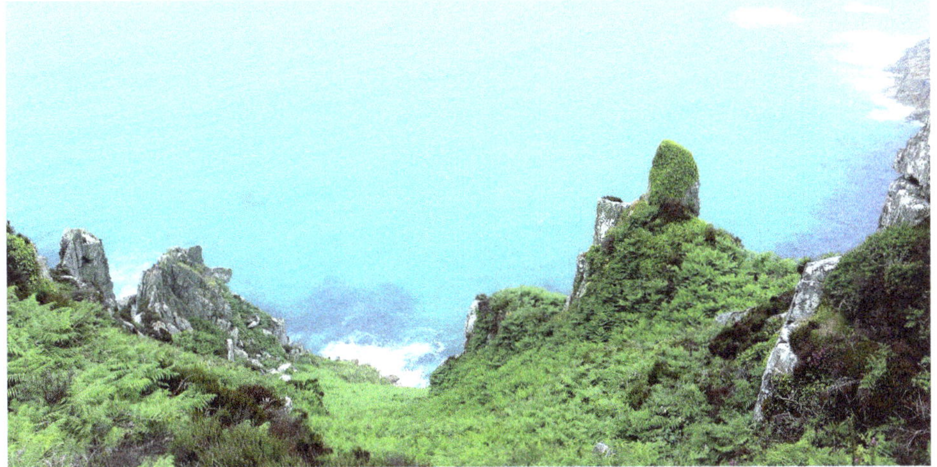

The beauty of the land meeting the turquoise ocean will astound you.

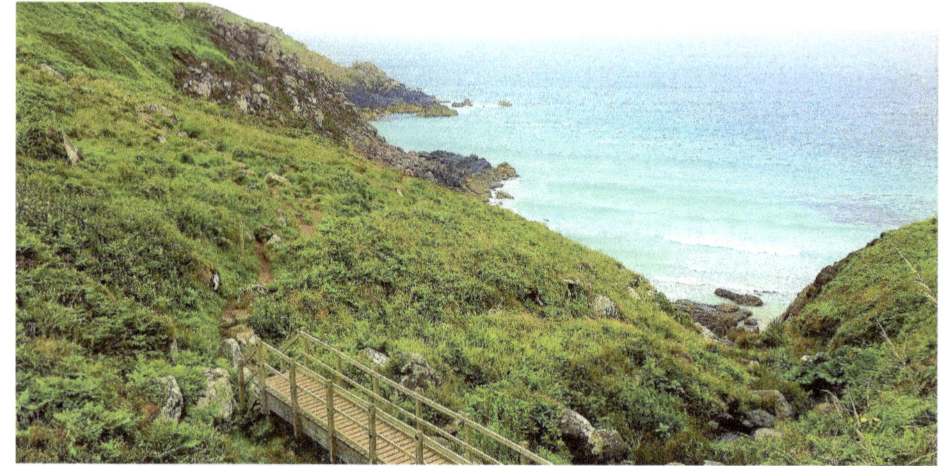

A small wooden footbridge used to span a ravine and stream.

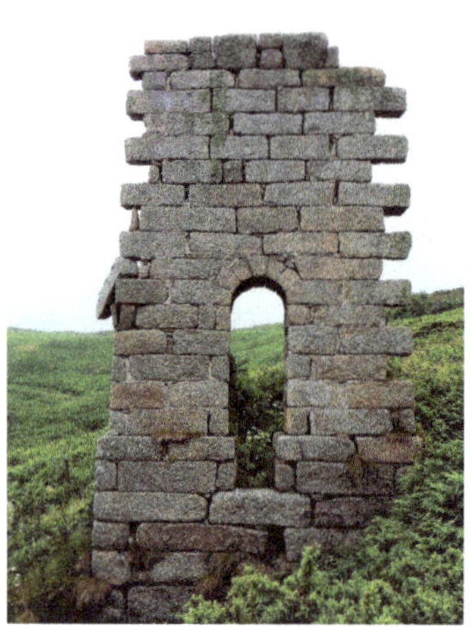

Signs of old mining.

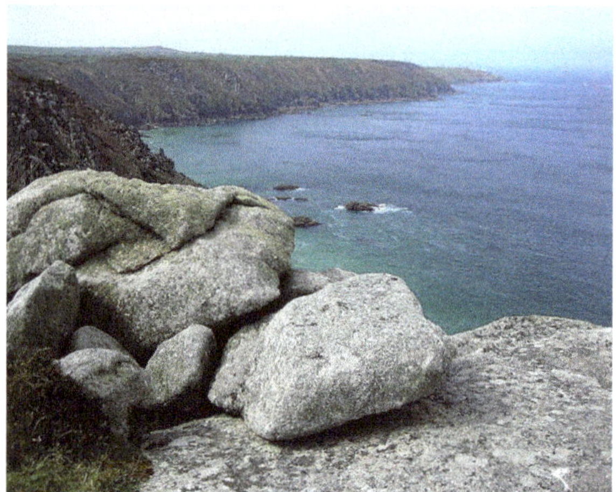

Breathtaking scenery.

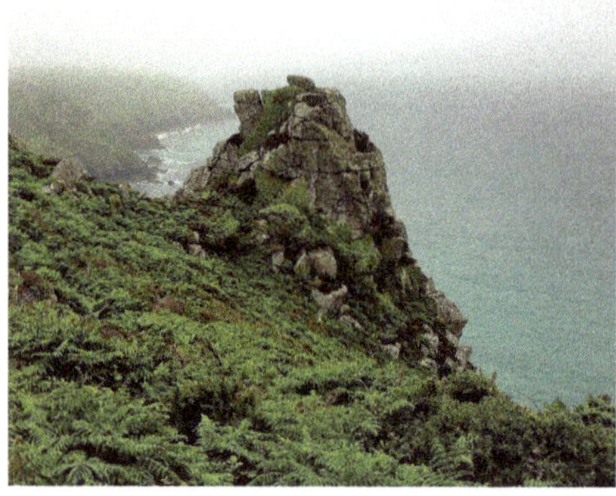

A misty morning on the coast path.

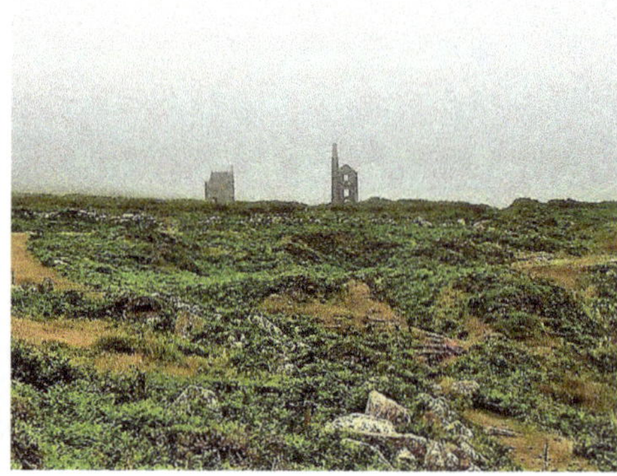

Old tin mines in the sea mist.

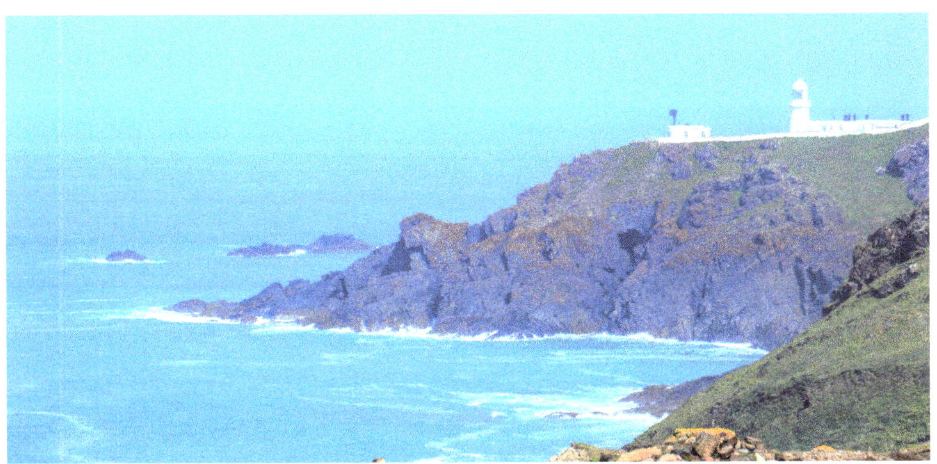

The magnificent Pendeen Watch Lighthouse.

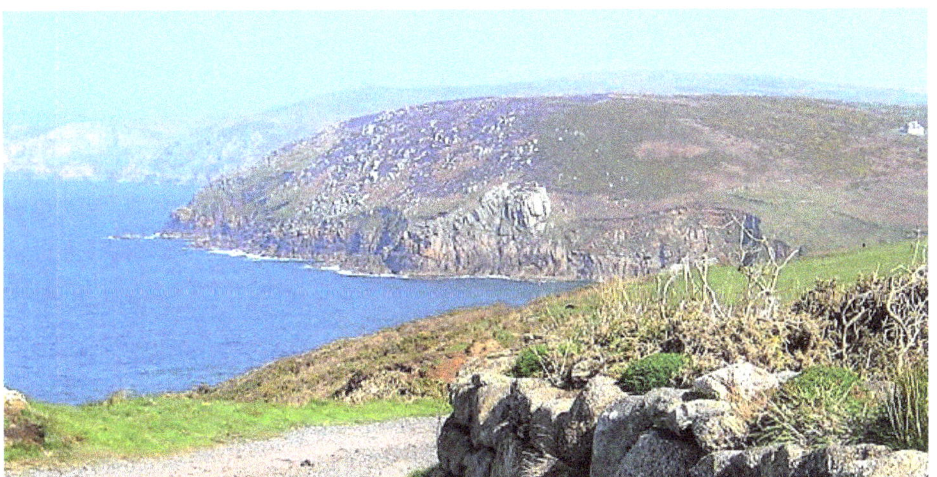

Beautiful sweeping coastline near Pendeen Watch.

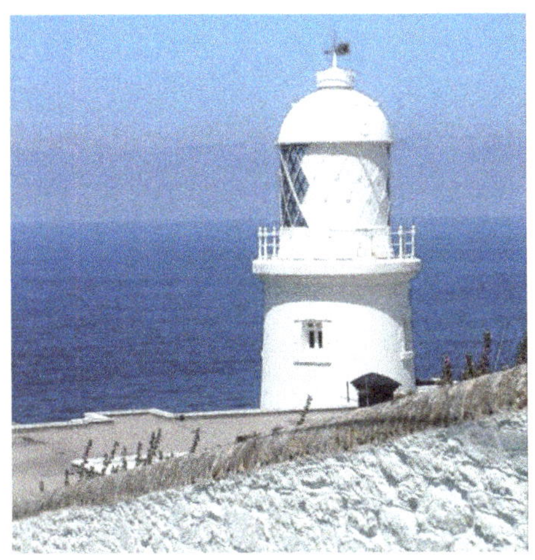

Pendeeen Watch Lighthouse.

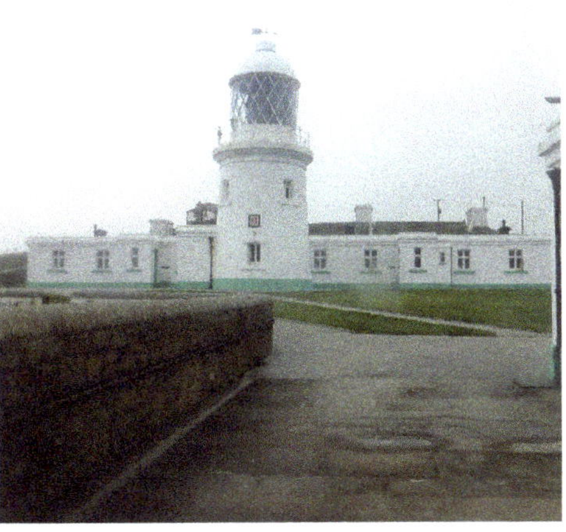

On a stormy day at Pendeen Watch.

Pendeen Watch to Cape Cornwall

This is a glorious section of the coastal path which has beautiful scenery, passes through the old tin mining areas of Levant and Bottalack, and ends at the incredible landscape of Cape Cornwall.

The Levant mine and beam engine is located within the St Just mining district, which is one of the most ancient mining areas in Cornwall. The mine shaft itself extends for over a mile under the seabed, which is testimony to the generations of mining which took place here.

The Crown Engine Houses at Botallack are a little further along the coast, which is probably the most photographed and loved of all of the old tin mining areas. The setting here is just breathtaking, and the contrast between the sea and the engine houses makes for a very beautiful and deeply romantic setting.

At the end of this section is the magnificent Cape Cornwall. This really is a stunning landscape, with dramatic views out to the Atlantic Ocean .The old mining chimney (The Heinz Monument) which stands proud on the summit of the cape, was kept as a monument to the local miners who toiled underground for many centuries in this area.

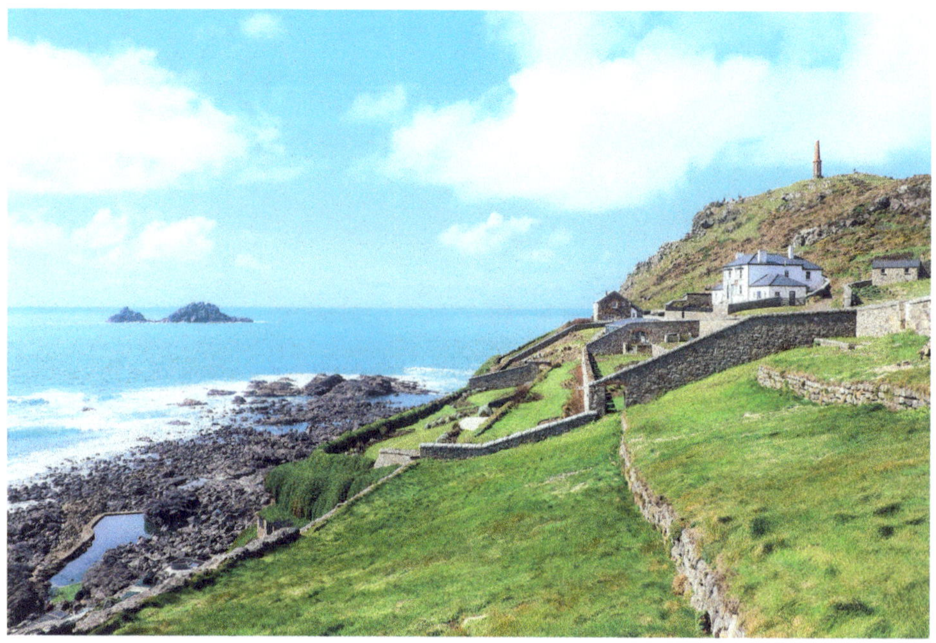

The magnificent Cape Cornwall,The Brisons can be seen out in the ocean.

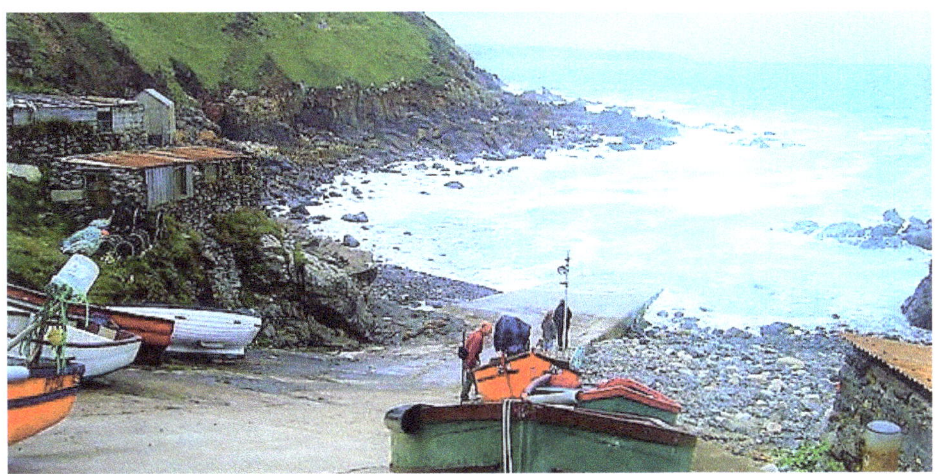

At Priests Cove, near Cape Cornwall.

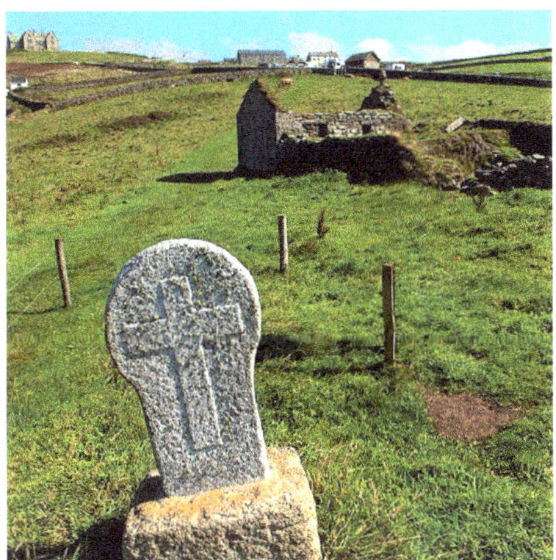

An old granite headstone.

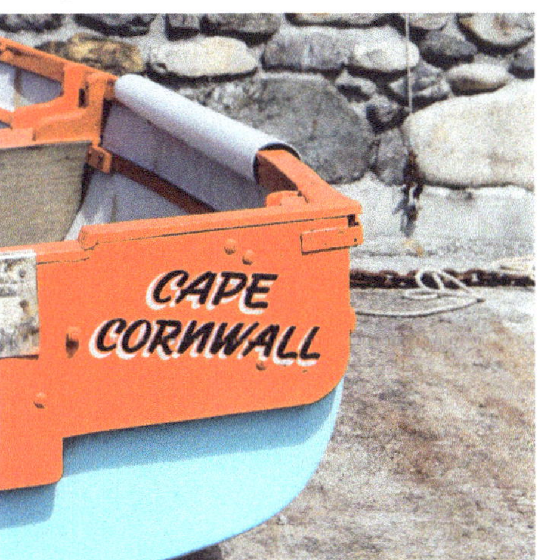

Lovely little boats at the harbour.

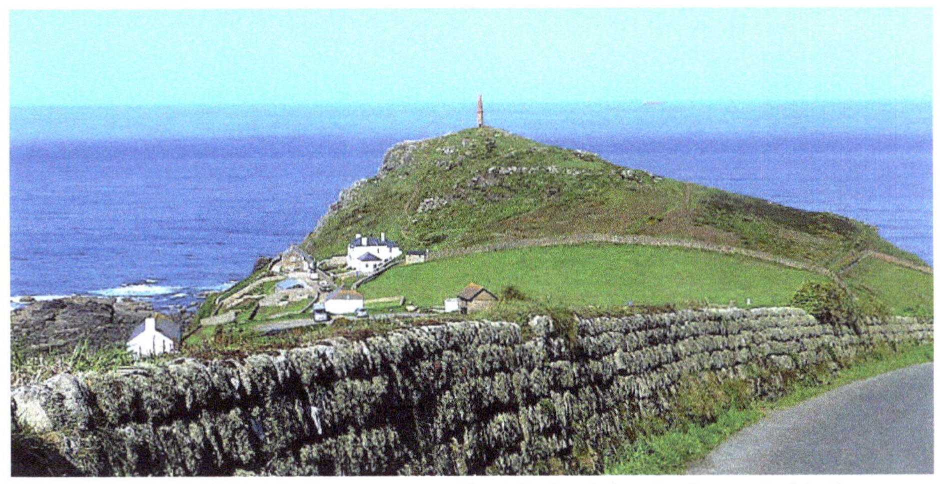

Looking down at Cape Cornwall with the Atlantic Ocean behind.

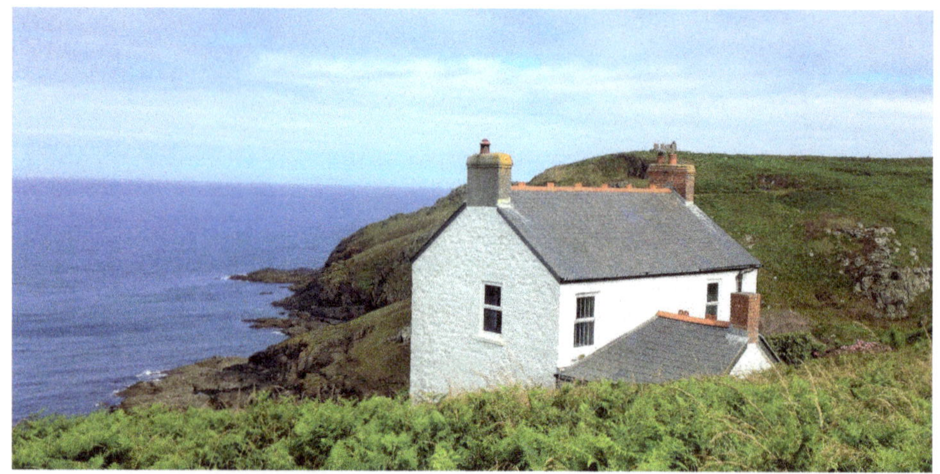

An old cottage near the Cape.

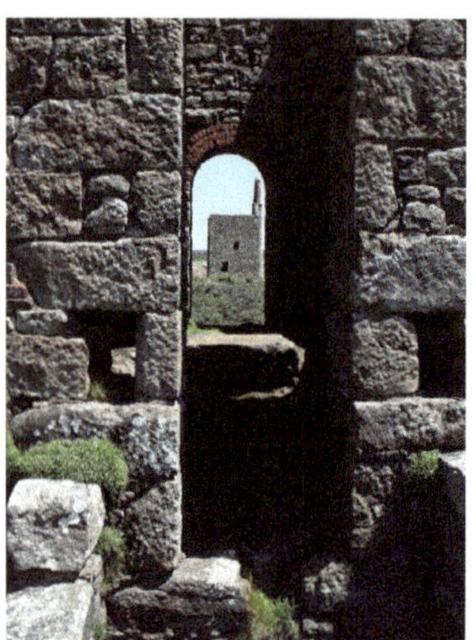

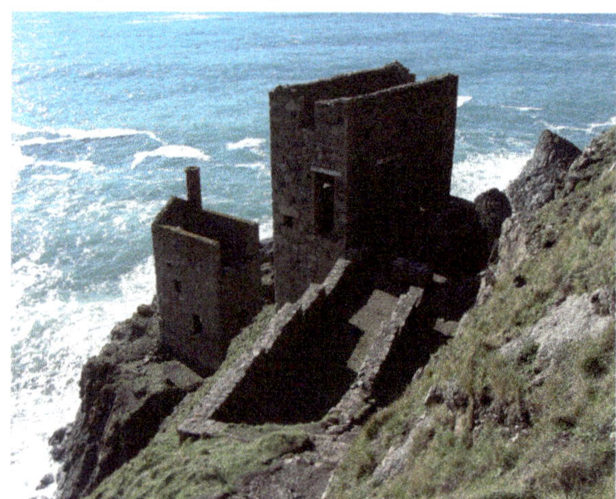

The Crown Engine Houses, Botallack.

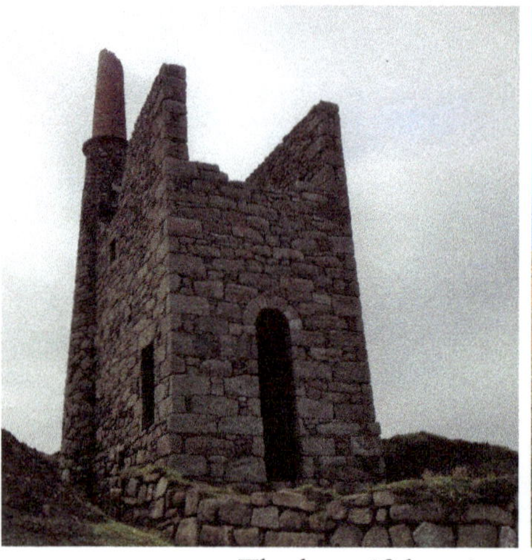

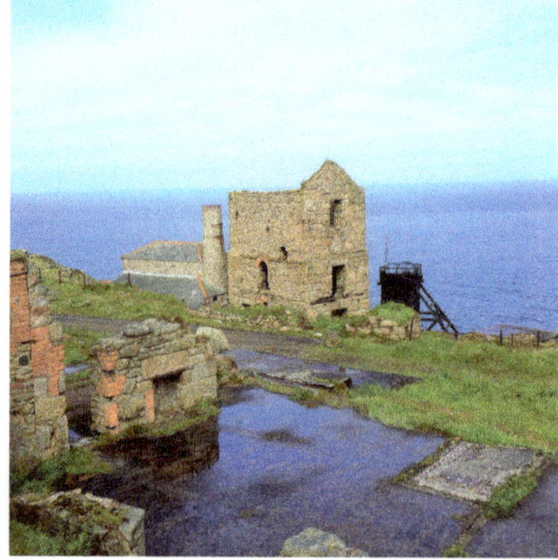

The beautiful setting of the Levant tin mines.

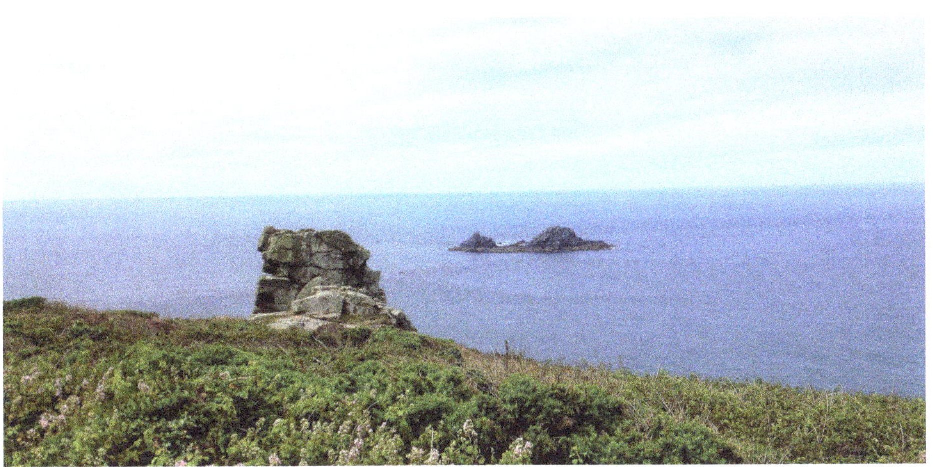

The Brisons which are 1 mile off of the coast near the Cape.

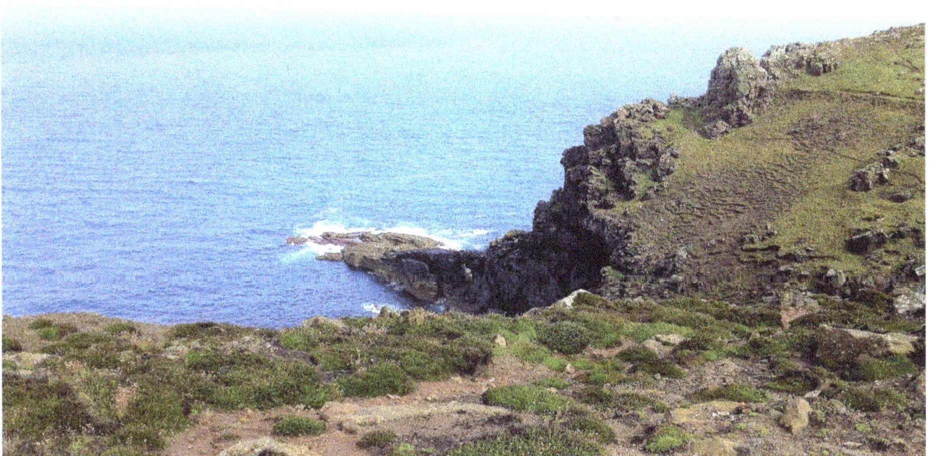

A stunning coastline meets the Atlantic Ocean.

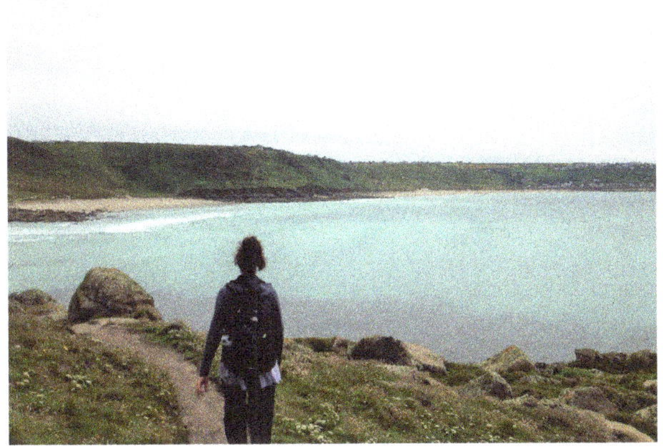

Breathtaking scenery.

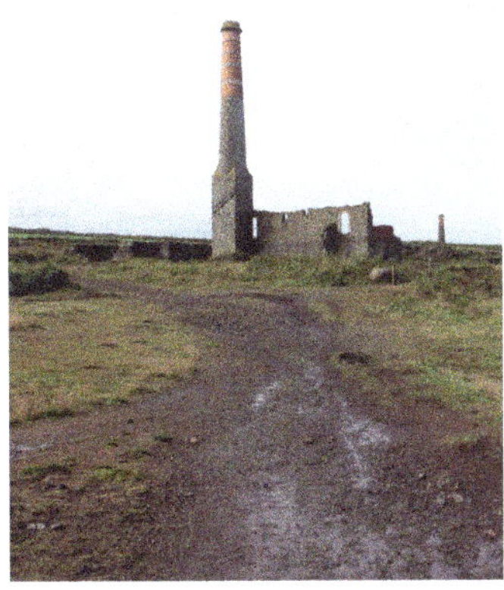

At Levant tin mines.

Cape Cornwall to Land's End to Porthcurno

This is a very diverse section of the coastline which is rich in history, with some interesting features and jaw-dropping coastal vistas.

After leaving Cape Cornwall the beautiful Whitesand Bay will emerge, with its fine sandy beach and crystal clear water. At the end of which is the popular little village of Sennen Cove.

Just along the coast is the famous landmark of Land's End which is a very popular tourist destination, especially during the summer months. This is the most south-westerly point of the British Isles, and as such the area attracts much interest. Incidentally, the most northerly is at John O'Groats in Scotland which is some 874 miles away.

The coast between Land's End and Porthcurno is much more remote and has some tremendous coastal scenery, with little coves and secluded beaches, which includes the beautiful Nanjizal Bay.

Turning the corner of the land at Gwennap Head the coastline now moves in an easterly direction. It passes by the stunning Porthgwarra before arriving at the world famous and totally unique Minack Theatre.

The Minack is the result of one woman's passion and love for the theatre, and for the stunning area which she lived in. Rowena Cade lived in the house which is perched on top of the adjacent tall cliffs and which overlooks the beautiful Porthcurno Bay. Rowena built the whole of this amazing theatre by hand, with the help of her trusty gardener.

It is true to say that this is her life's work as she toiled over the construction of the Minack for decades. You can really sense the love that she put into it, as the theatre and setting are completely breathtaking. The first staged production at the Minack was in 1929 when a group of local players performed 'A Midsummer Night's Dream', the theatre hasn't looked back and is still going strong today.

This section ends at the absolutely beautiful setting of Porthcurno with its gorgeous sandy beach, and which also has the impressive Horrace Headland and Logan Rock as the bays backdrop. Logan means 'rocking' in old Cornish, and the large rock which is perched on top of the headland rocks slightly in the wind. This is quite miraculous as the rock weighs in at 80 tons.

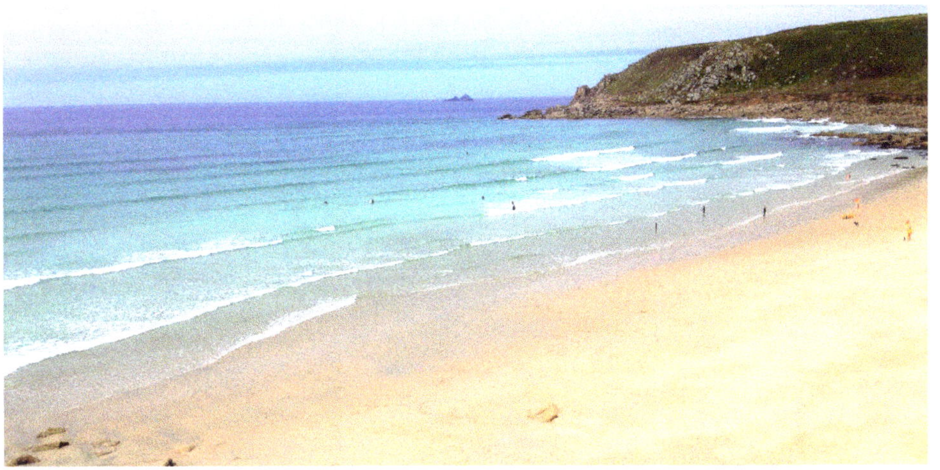

The picturesque Whitesand Bay, Sennon Cove.

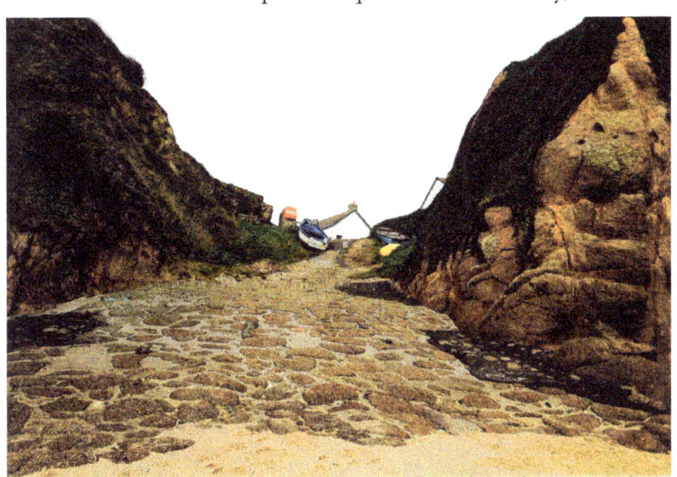

Looking up from the beach at Porthgwarra.

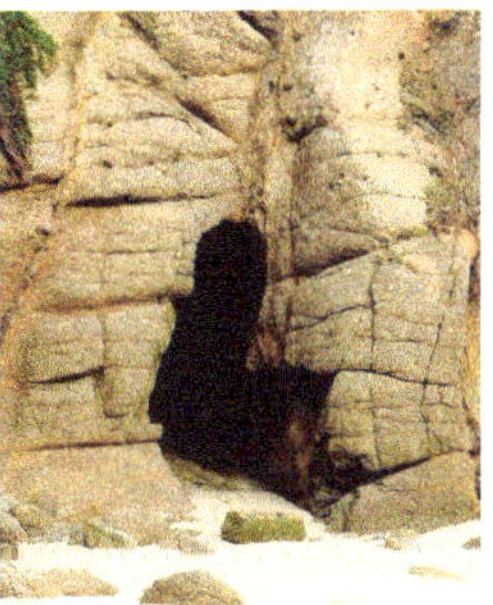

A cave in the rocks.

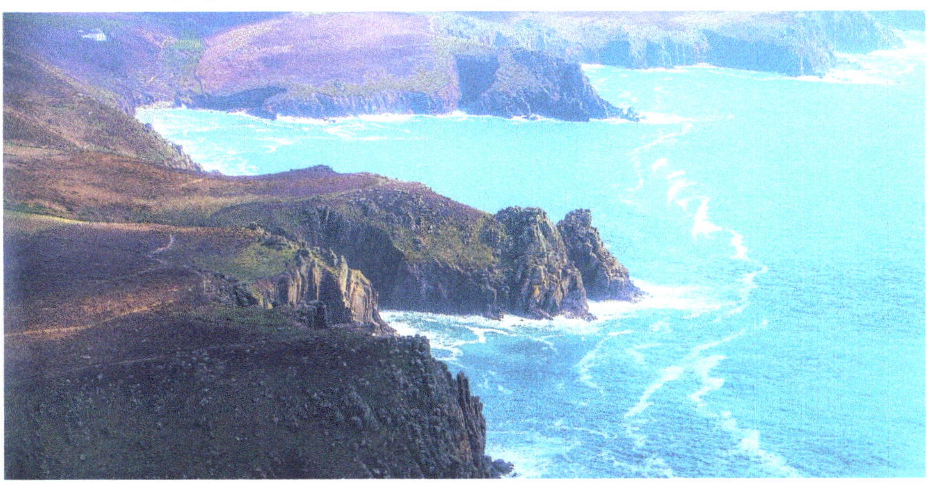

Beautiful blue sea meets the rugged coastline.

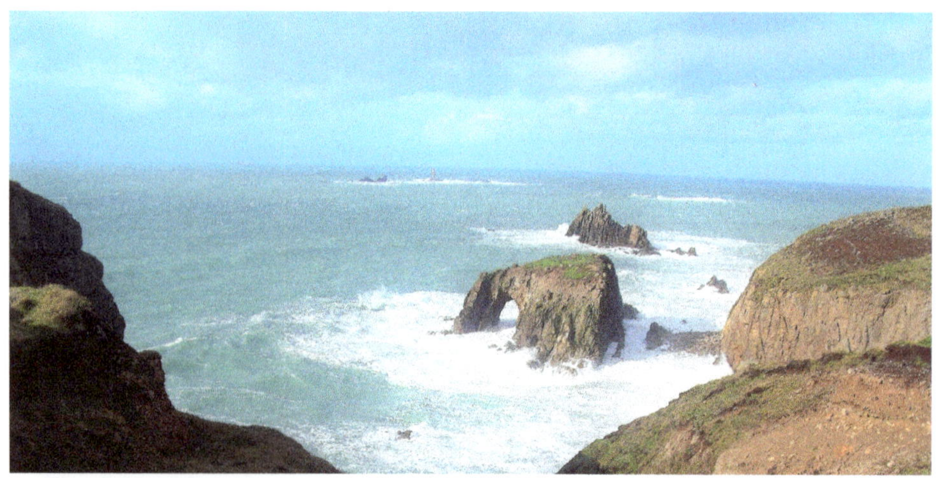

The Armed Knight, Enys Dodnan and Longships Lighthouse in the distance.

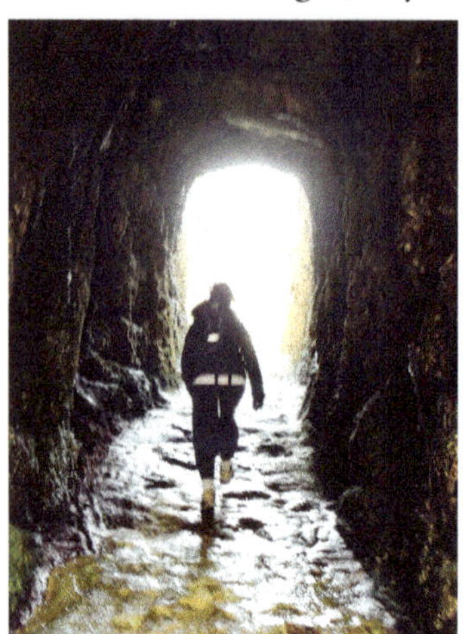

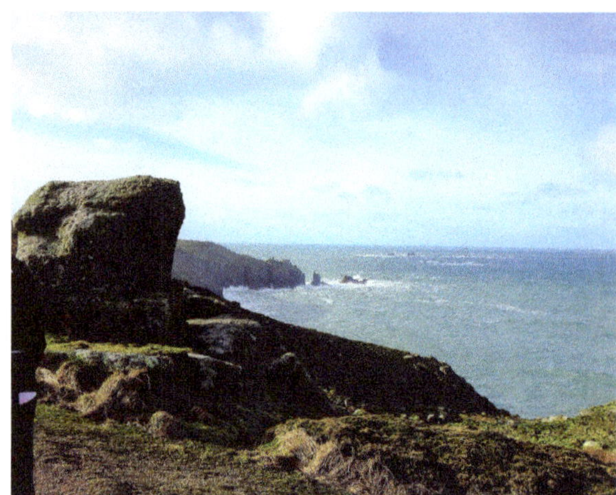

Stunning coves with caves to explore.

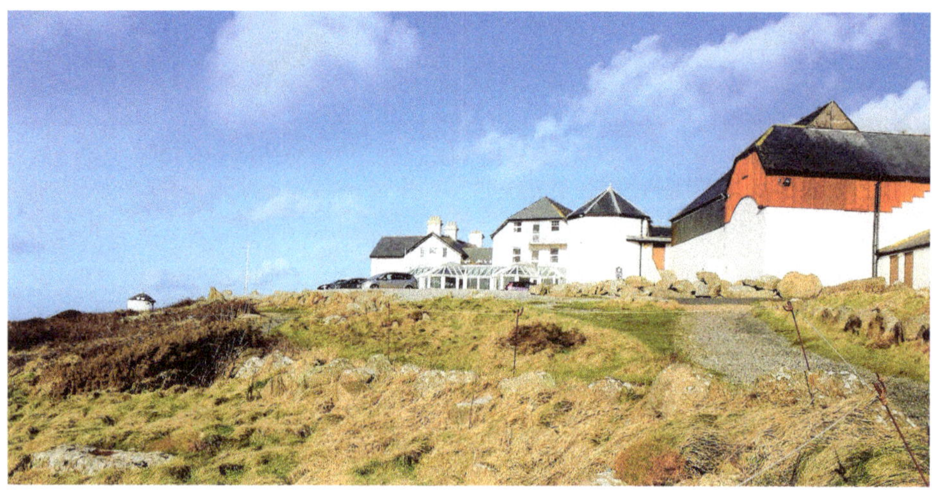

The Land's End Hotel.

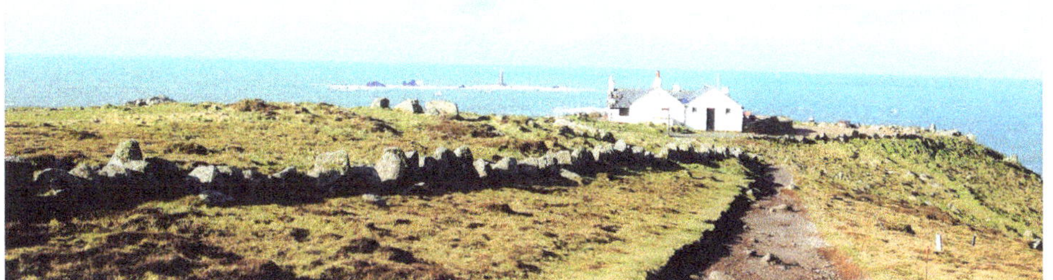

Land's End with Longships Lighthouse behind.

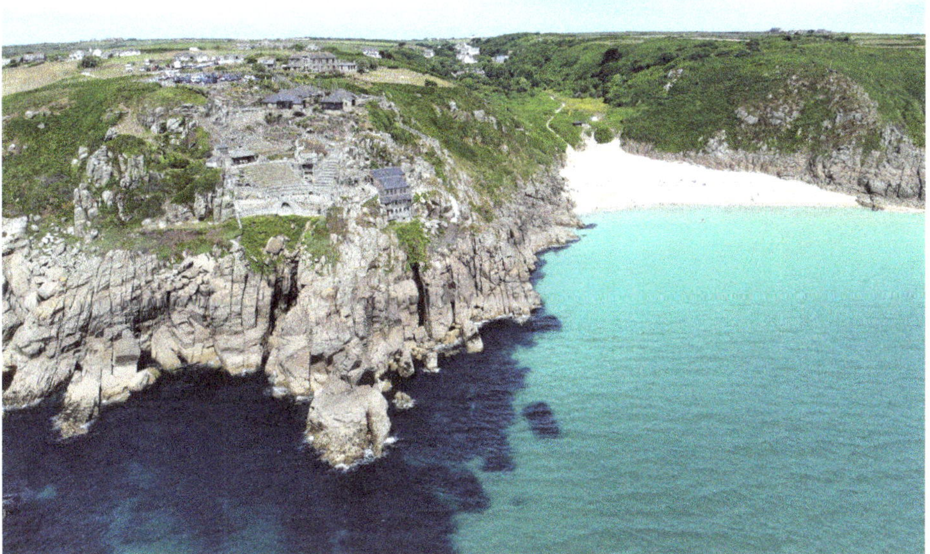

Porthcurno with the Minack Theatre to the left.

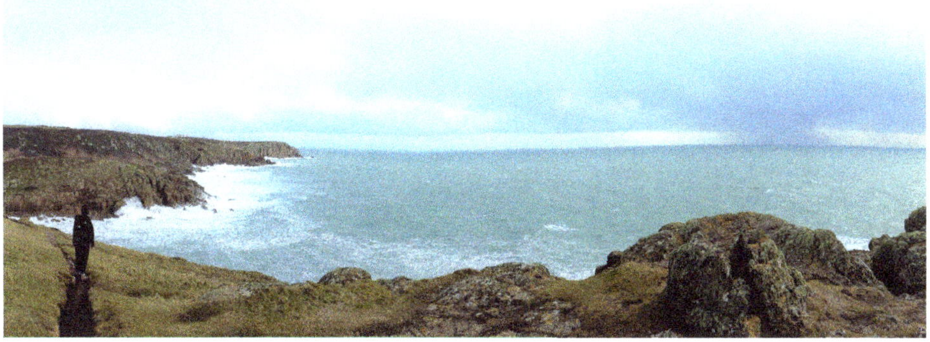

Amazing coastal landscapes.

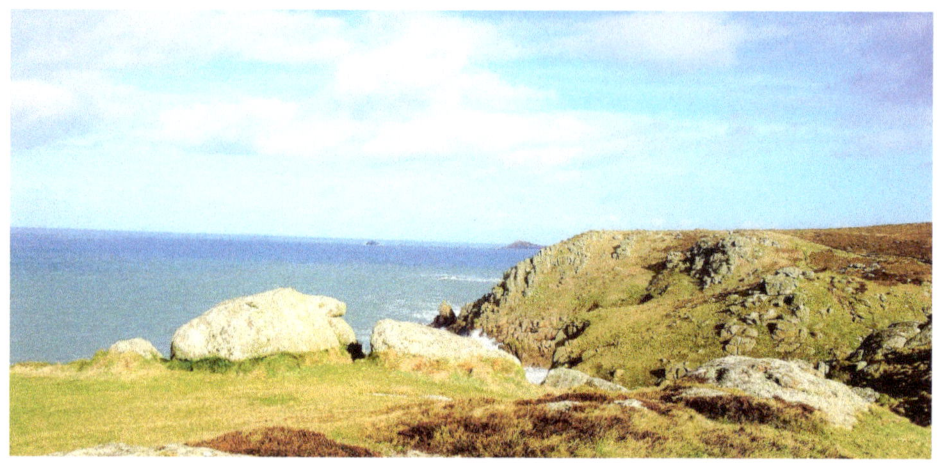

The solitude of the coast is apparent between Land's End and Porthcurno.

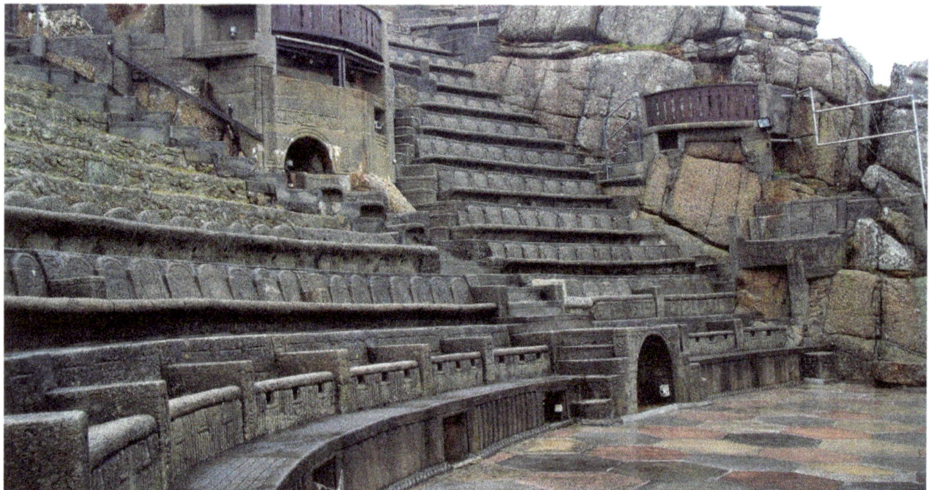

The Minack Theatre on a stormy day.

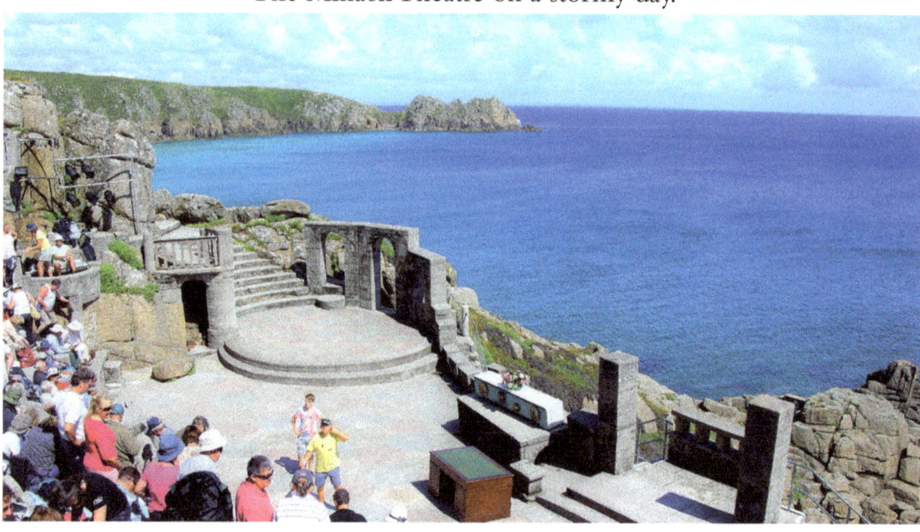

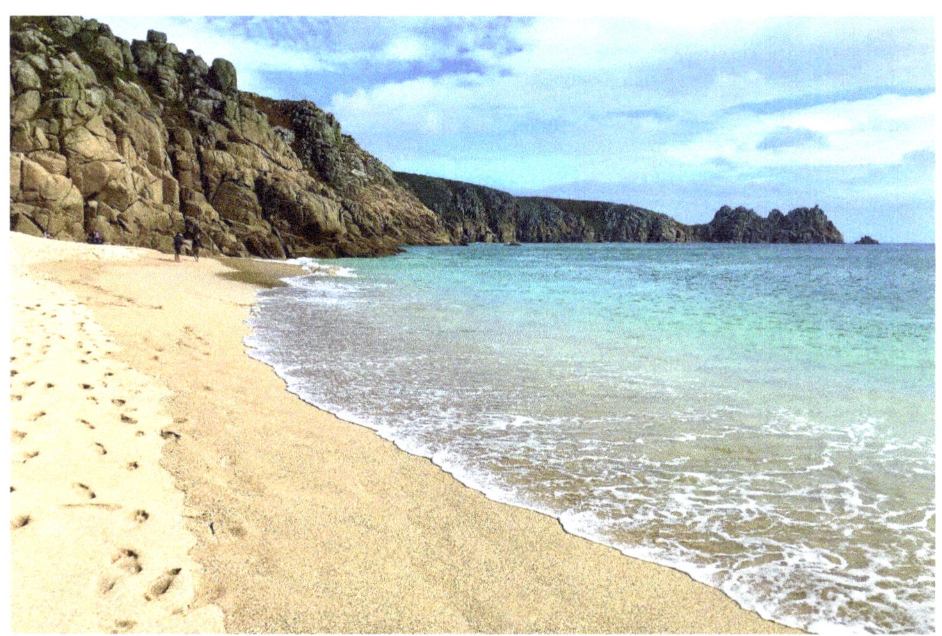

Porthcurno's breathtaking beach with Logan Rock behind.

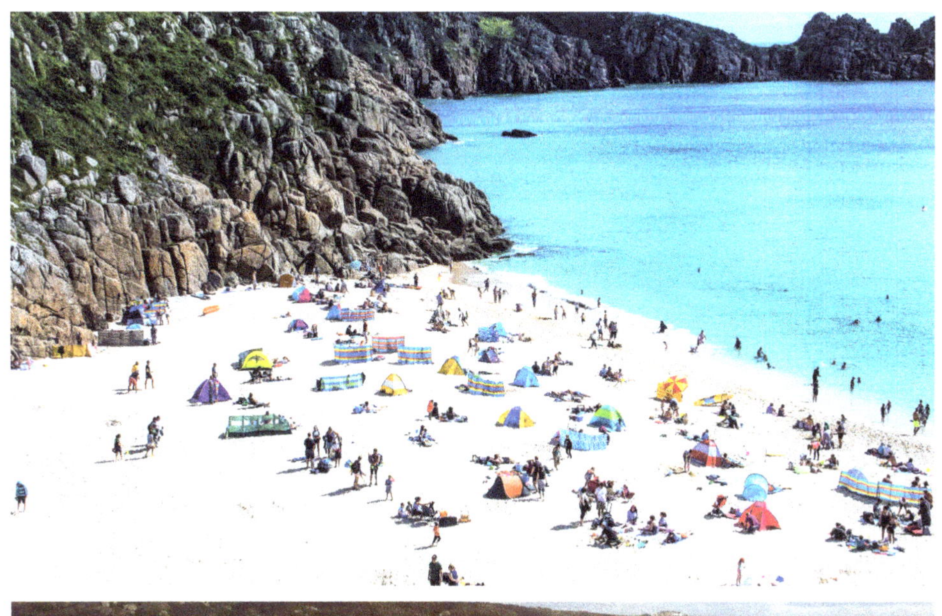

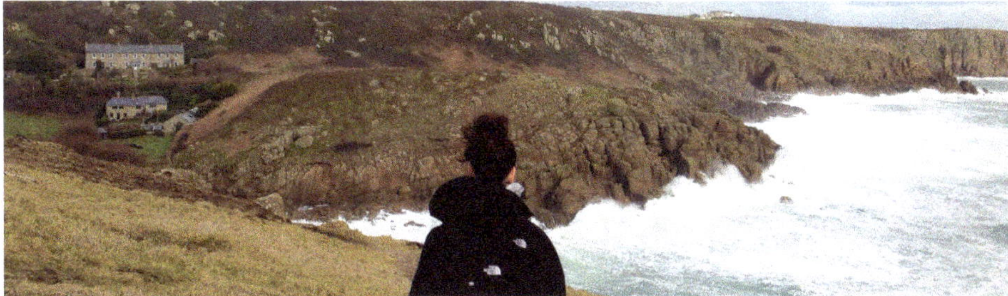

Porthcurno to Marazion

This is a very diverse section of the West Cornwall coastline, with a rich history and every type of beauty that you would expect to see when circumnavigating the Cornish coast.

After leaving the scenic setting of Porthcurno the views become more desolate and rugged again, with some stunning little coves and magnificent headlands.

The next little settlement is at Penberth Cove which has an extremely attractive fishing harbour, with one of the most iconic houses along the Cornish coastline perched just above it. This tiny fishing hamlet and cove is stunning, and is sandwiched between the foot of a wooded valley and the turquoise water of the sea. Next to this hamlet is Cribba Head with its amazing views across the jagged coastline.

After passing by the rocky beach at St Loy, the coast winds its way around to the village of Lamorna with its large cove and harbour. The harbour wall at Lamorna was built in 1850 to meet the demands of local industry, which included vast amounts of local stone quarrying.

The village and fishing port of Mousehole (pronounced Mous'all) is a few miles further along the coast with its delightful little harbour and quaint old cottages. This is a very beautiful area and its long history with the ocean is very evident. Every Christmas the locals erect decorations around the harbour walls, which is very pretty and warming to see in the dark and cold of winter.

Next to Mousehole is one of Cornwall's busiest fishing harbours. Newlyn has been a hub of fishing in the area since the late 17th century and this is clearly seen as you stroll through its old streets.

Merging with Newlyn is the town of Penzance which is the most westerly town in Cornwall, and with a population of around 21000 people it is one of the largest towns in the area.

At the end of the large sweeping bay at Penzance, the beautiful village of Marazion emerges, with the iconic St Michaels Mount standing proud just off of the coast. The medieval castle and church at St Michaels Mount sit on top of a tidal island, which means that at low tide you are able to walk out to this most stunning of Cornish landmarks.

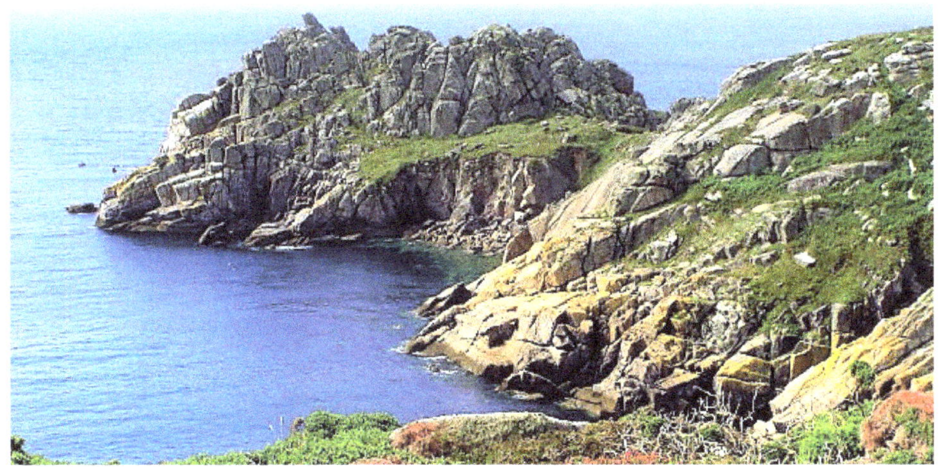
Looking back at Horrace Headland and Logan Rock.

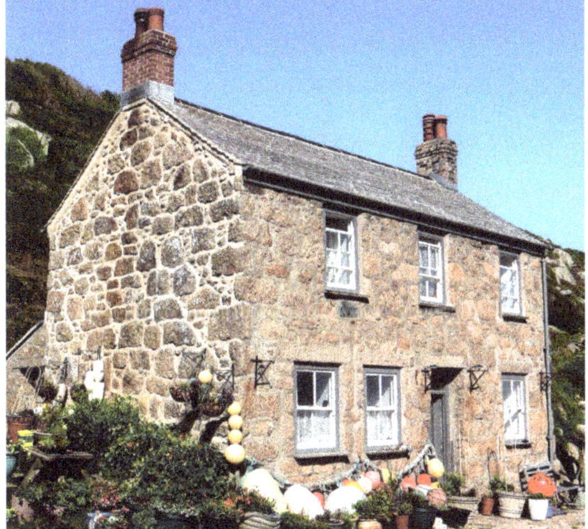
The Fisherman's cottage at Penberth Cove.

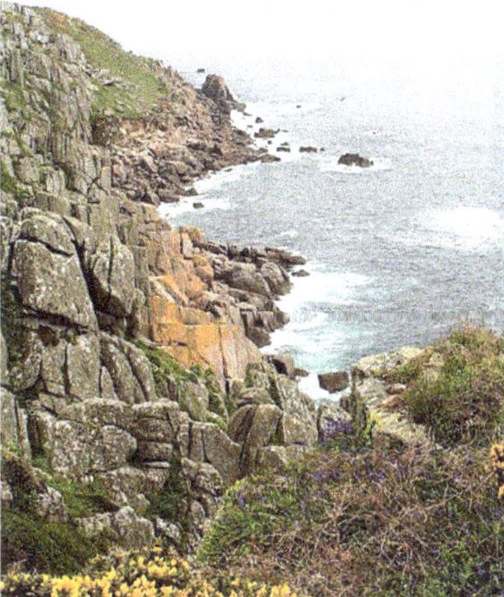
Overlooking Coffin Rock

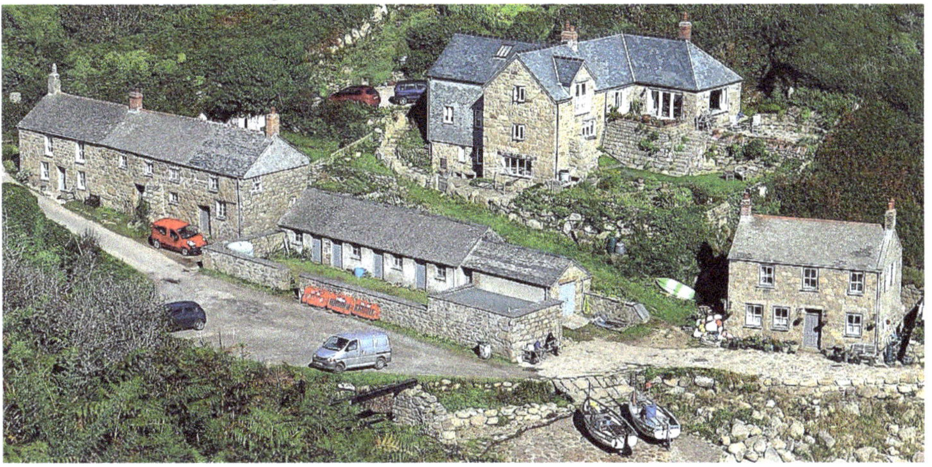
The picturesque Penberth Cove.

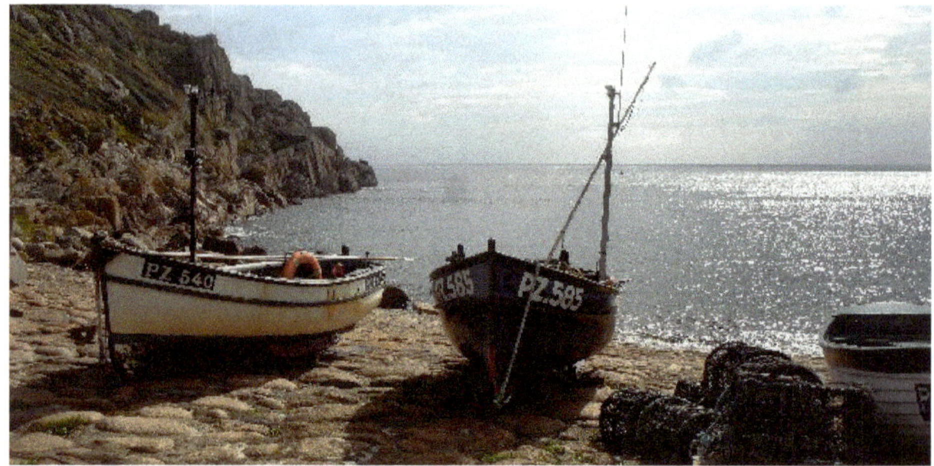

Fishing boats and lobster pots at Penberth Cove.

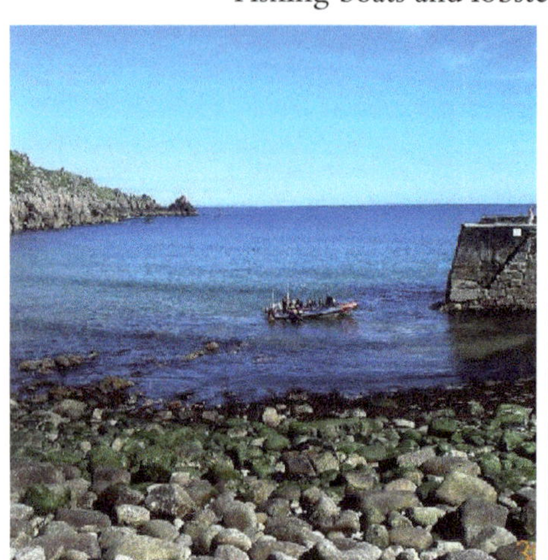

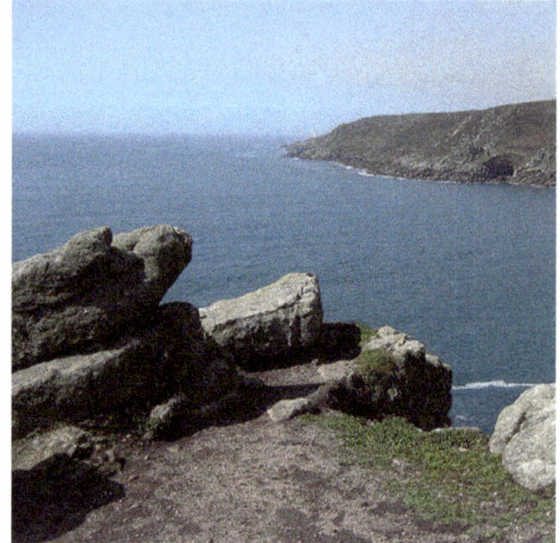

Lamorna Cove.

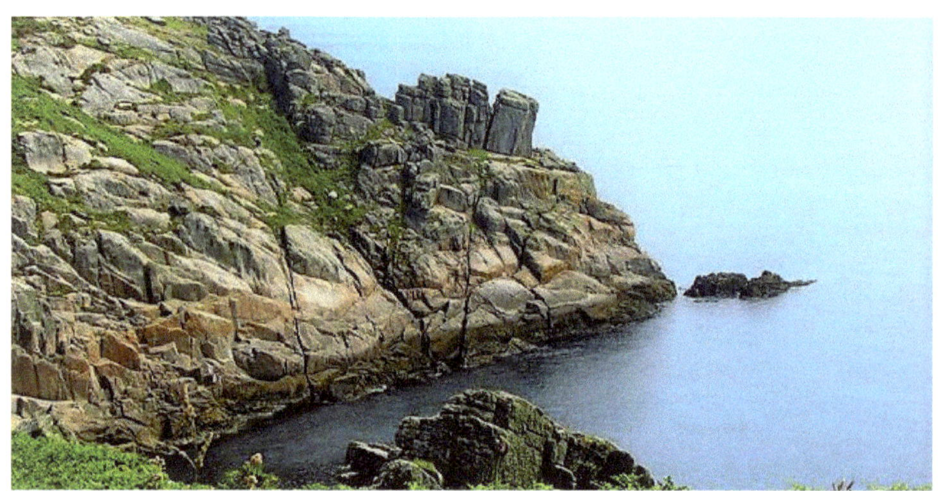

At Cribba Head.

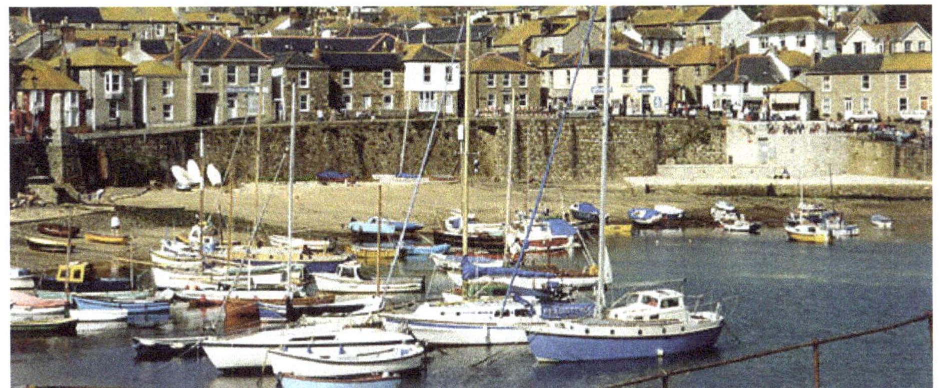

Mousehole Harbour.

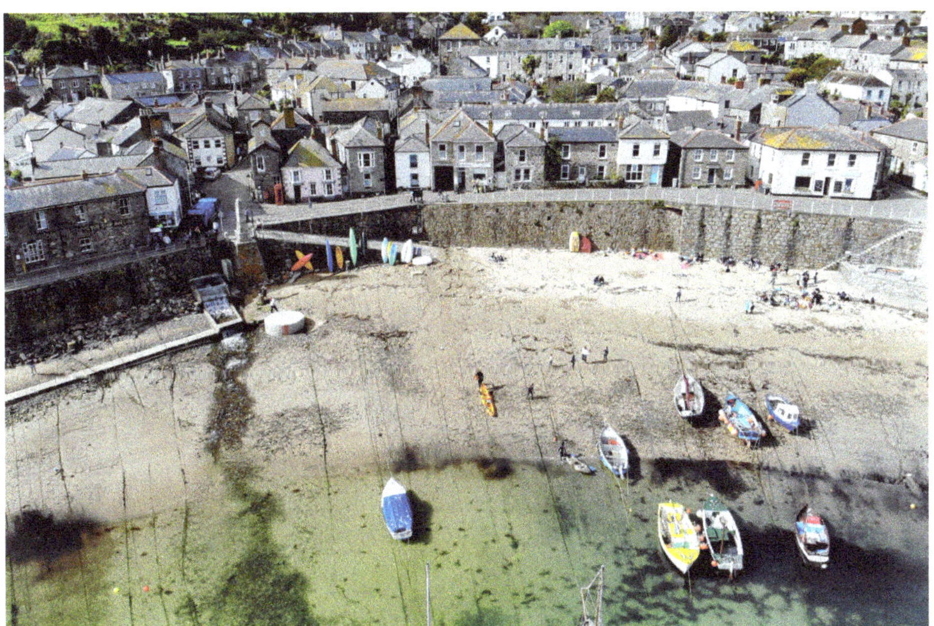

The stunning harbour and village of Mousehole.

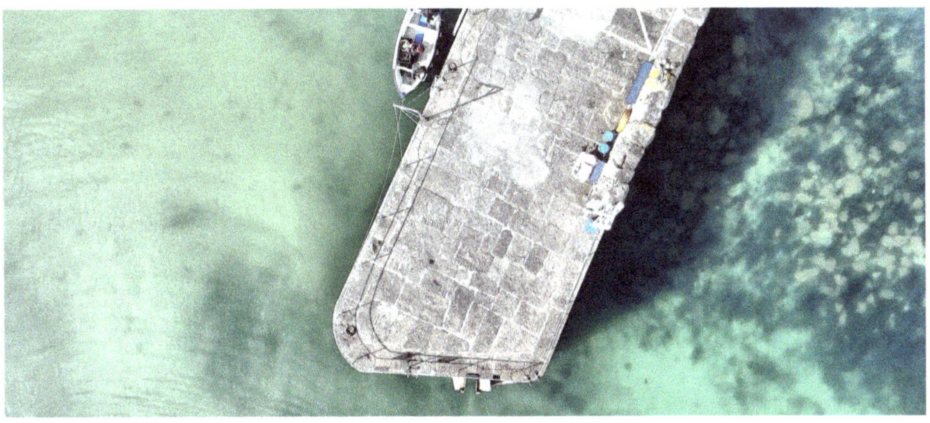

Aerial photograph of Mousehole Harbour, with crystal clear water.

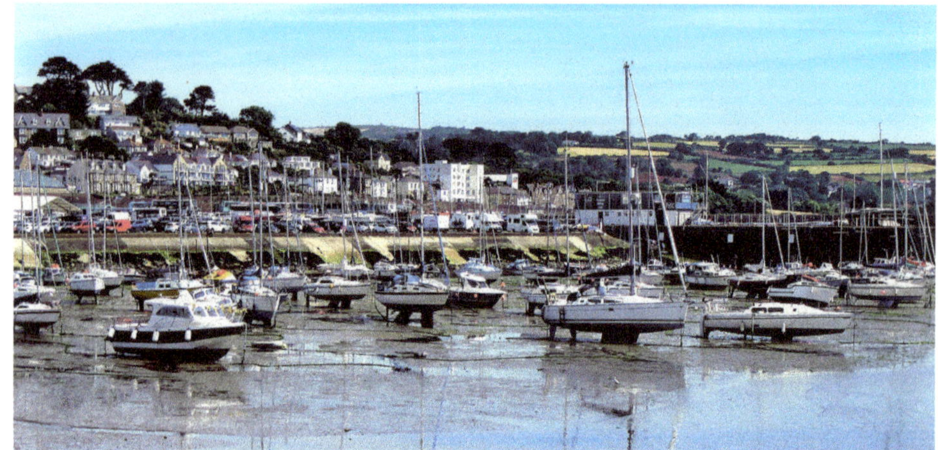

Boats moored at Penzance Harbour.

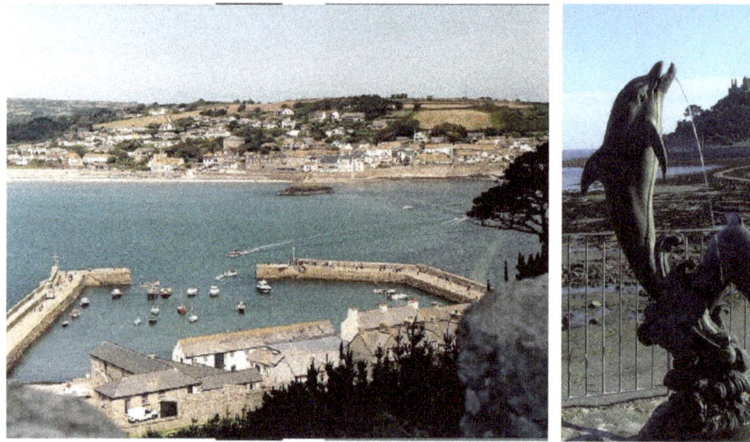

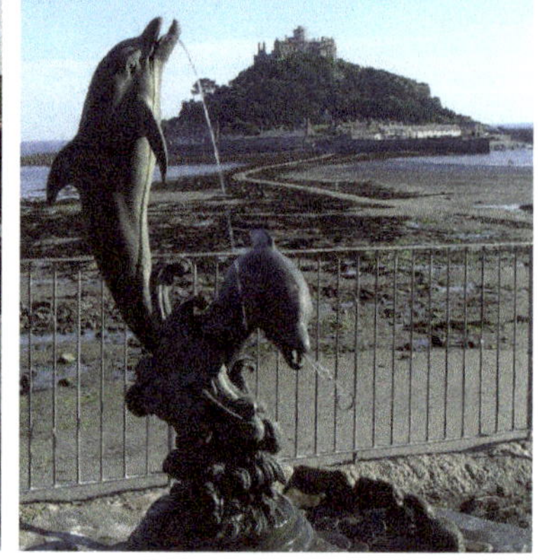

Above and below: The ancient market town of Marazion.

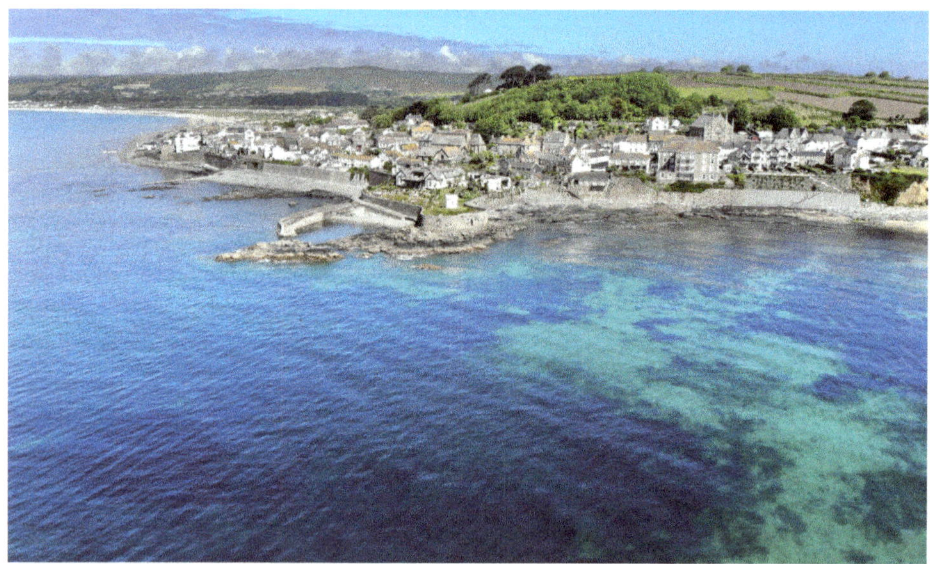

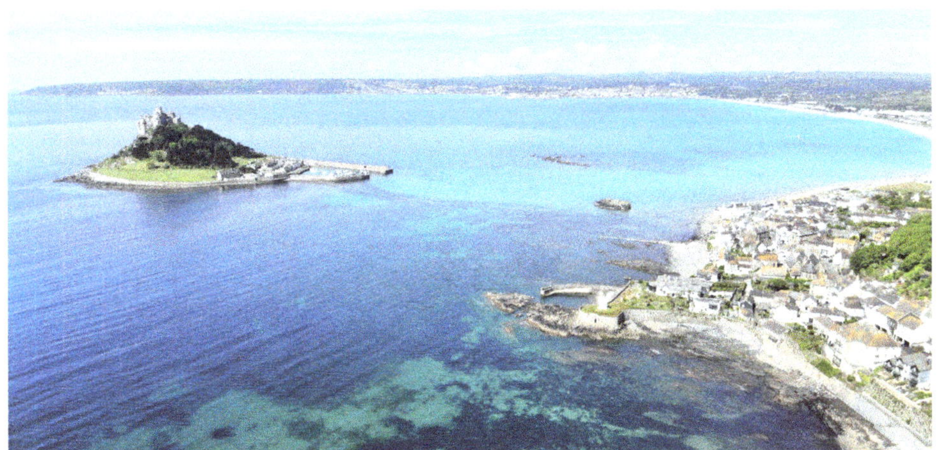

Above: St Michael's Mount and Marazion.

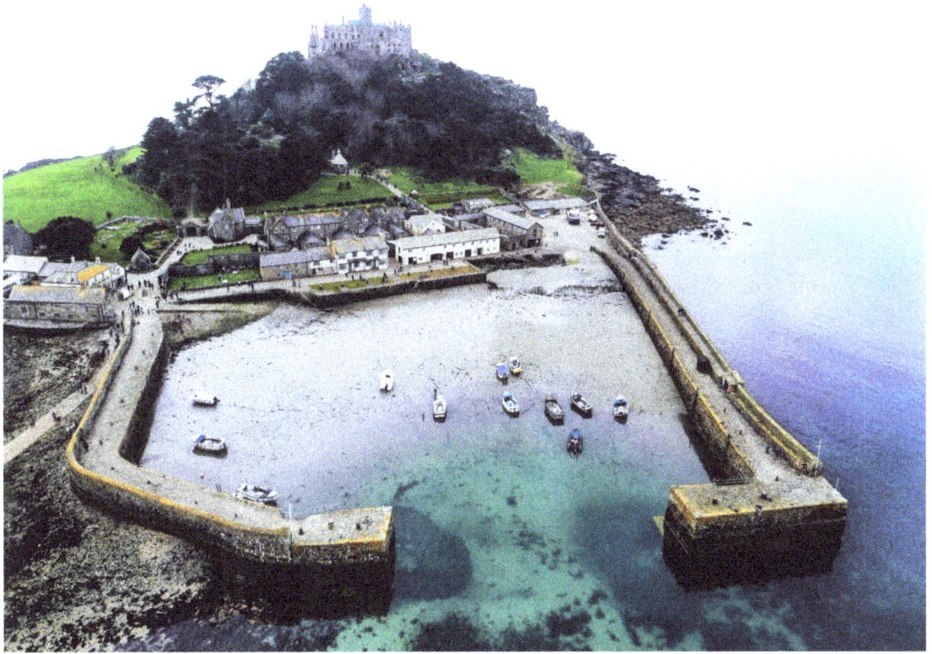

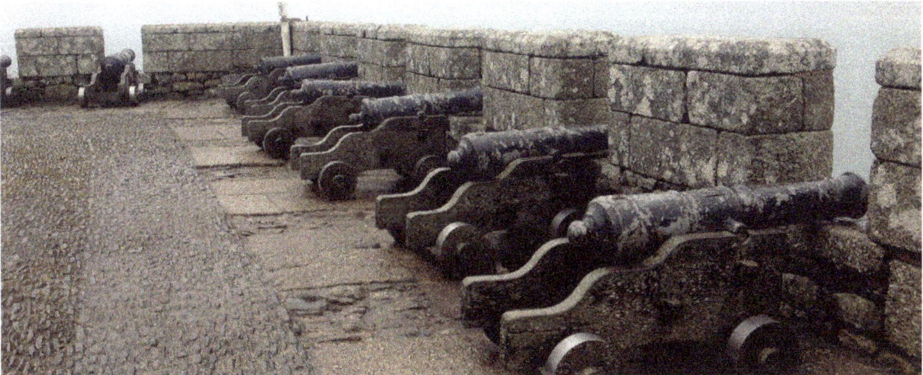

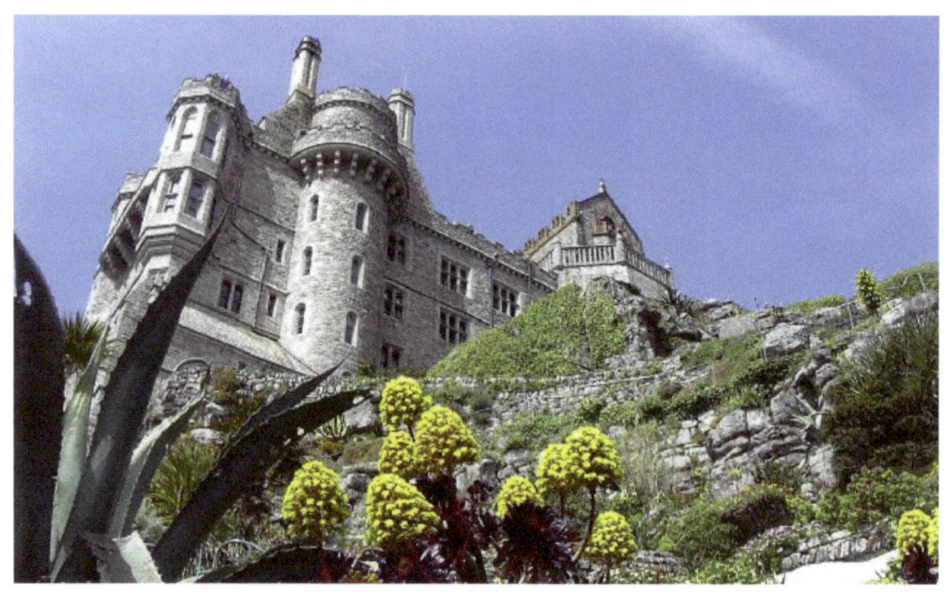

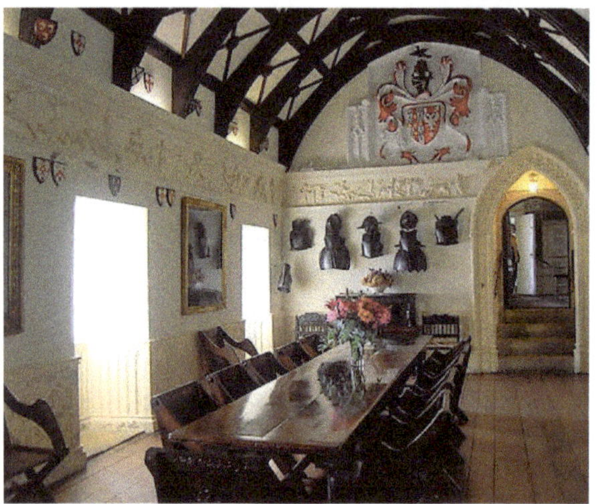

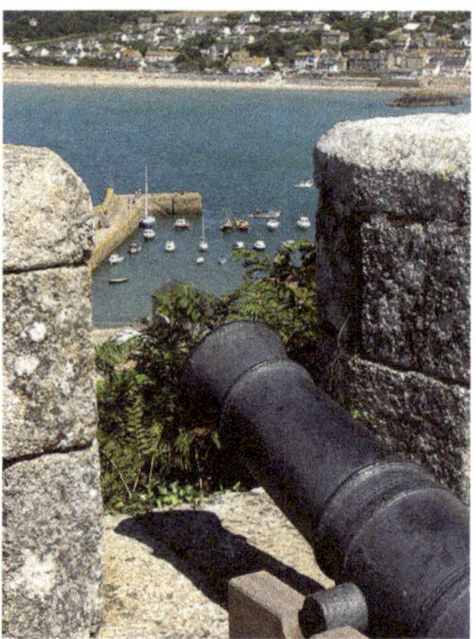

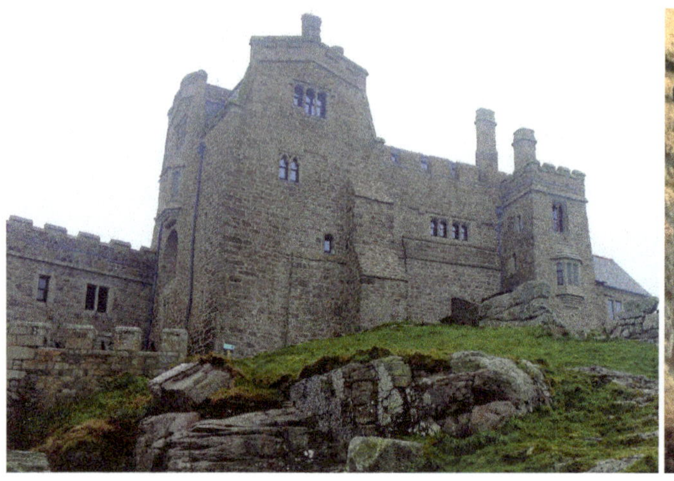

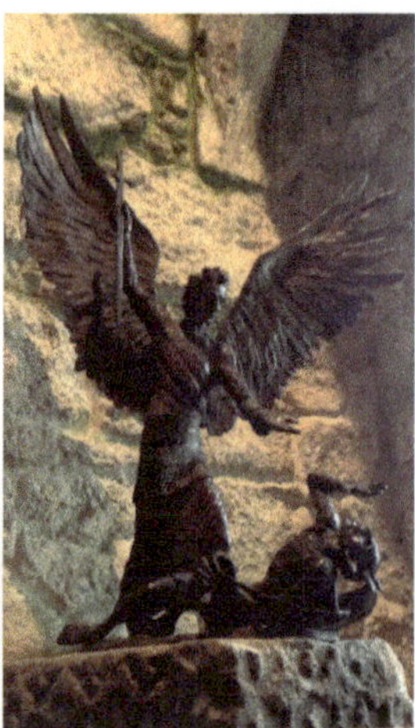

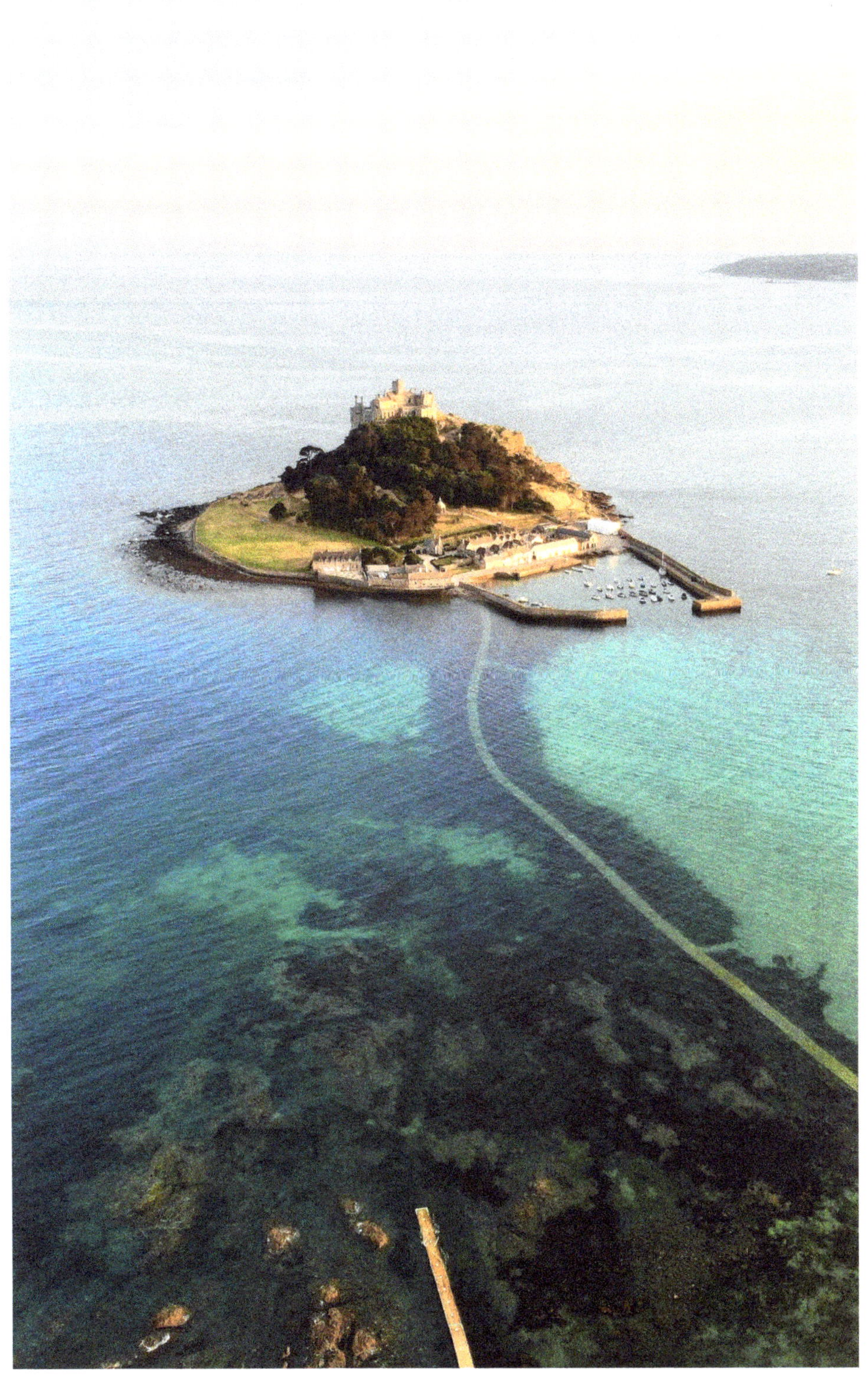

Marazion to Porthleven

From Marazion the coastline starts to turn in a southerly direction, however this is more prominent on the next section as the coast edges its way down to Lizard Point.

Between Marazion and Porthleven the coast is littered with little coves and beaches, which are broken up by the prominent headlands of Cudden Point, Hoe Point and Trewavas Head.

The beautiful beaches of Perran Sands, Kenneggy Sands, Praa Sands and Porthleven Sands are all in a line on this part of the West Cornish coast. On a summers day, their bright golden sand glows as it touches the rich blues of the ocean, making for a delightful section of the coast which is popular with the local sun worshippers.

Like many of Cornwall's coastal settlements, Porthleven was once a little fishing village which nestled into the shelter of a wooded valley in Mount's Bay. The name of the town is thought to be derived from 'St Elvan' and is associated with St Breaca, the patron saint of the nearby coastal village of Breage.

From the historic harbour at Porthleven, its sandy beach runs east for another three glorious miles. Halfway along its length is the fantastic Loe Bar, where the sand becomes the divide between the ocean and a large inland lake of fresh water.

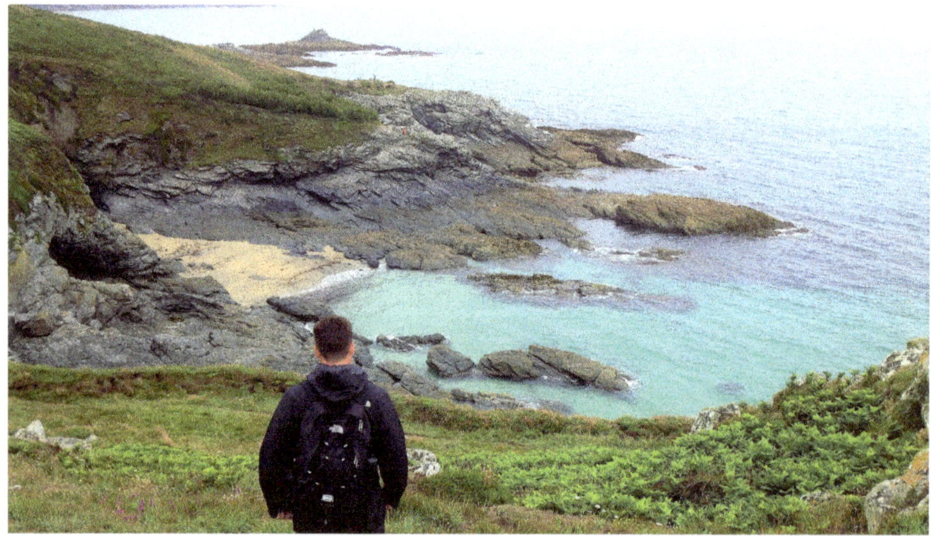

Walking down to a sandy cove with turquoise sea.

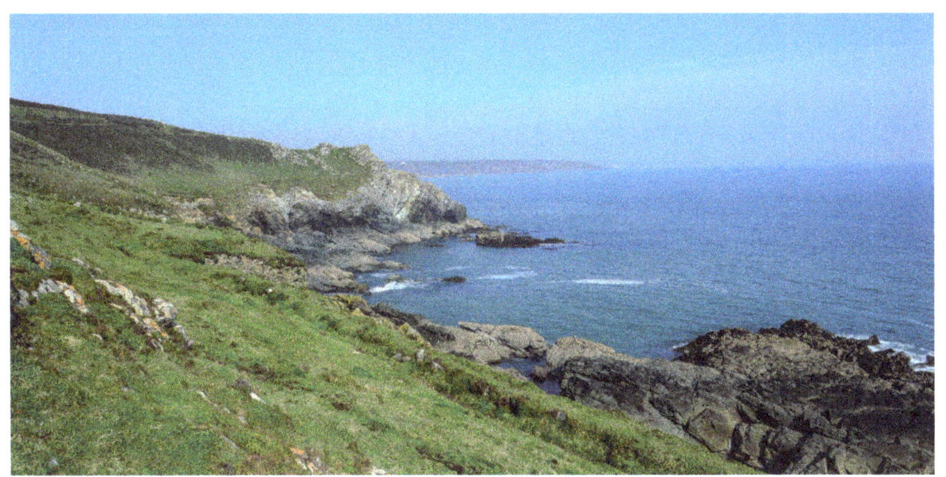

At Cudden Point, looking towards the Lizard.

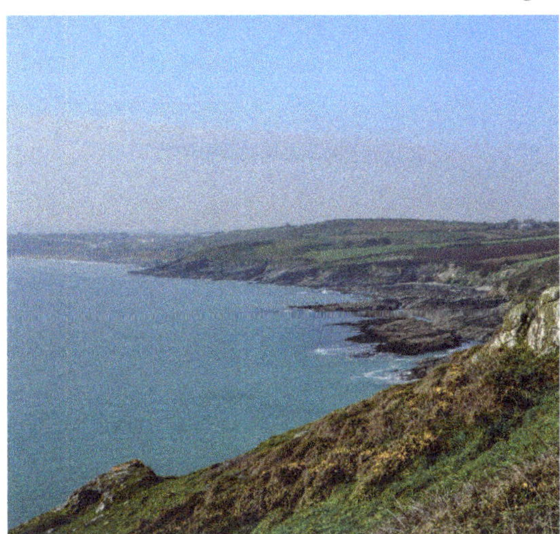

At Cudden Point, looking to Perran Sands.

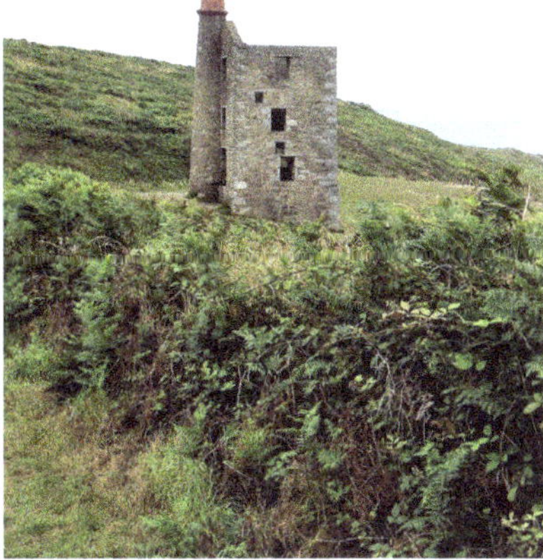

An old tin mine at Trewavas Head.

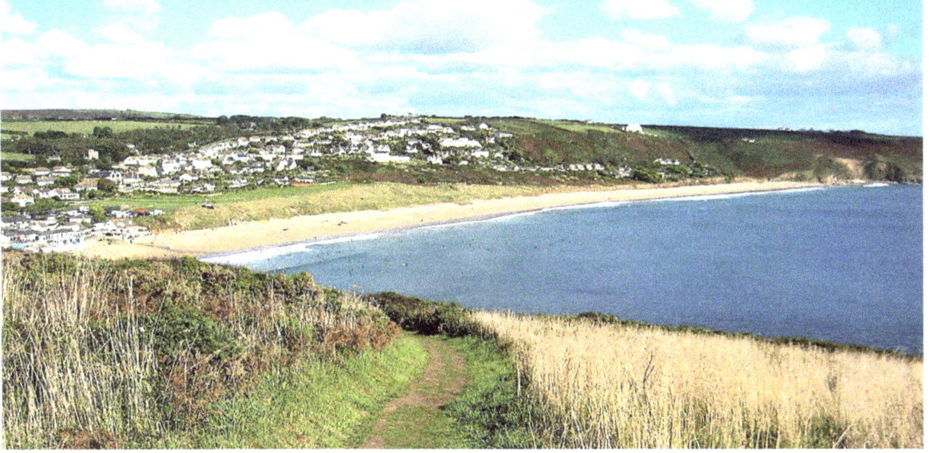

The picturesque Praa Sands.

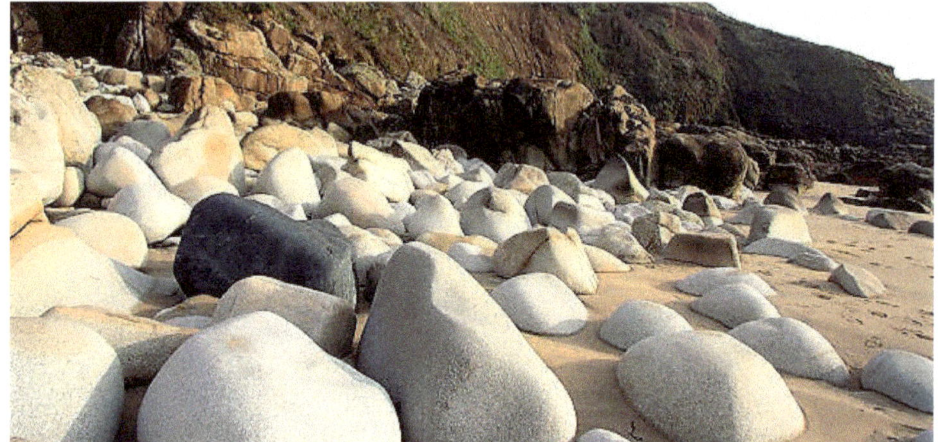
Rocks on the beach at the end of Praa Sands.

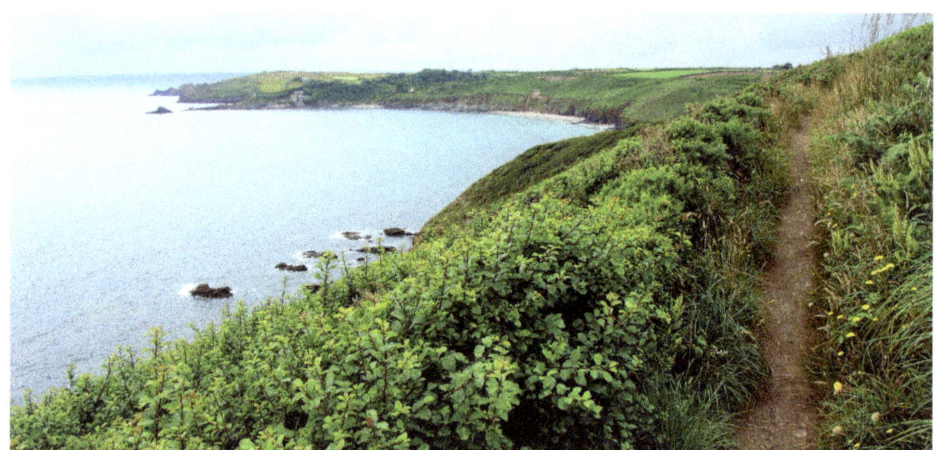
The South West Coast Path near Praa Sands.

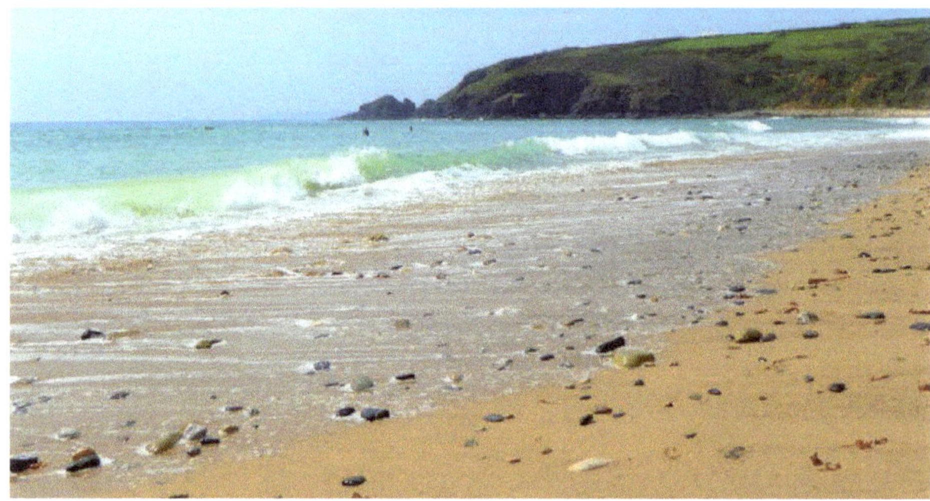
The blue surf crashing into Praa Sands.

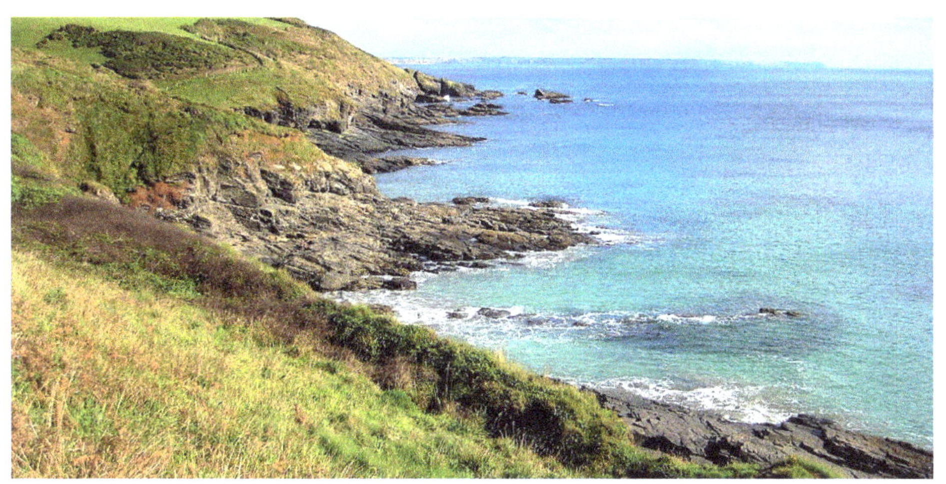
The coastline after Praa Sands.

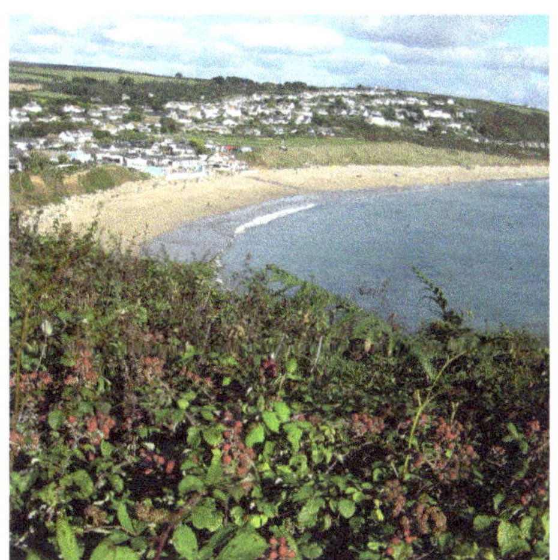
Praa Sands.

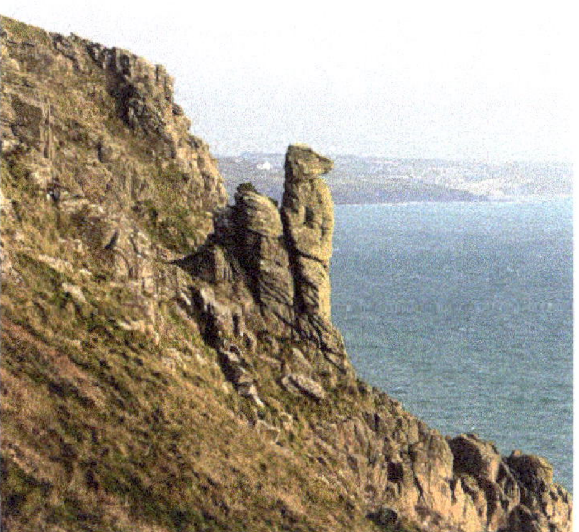
The 'camel' rock formation at Trewavas.

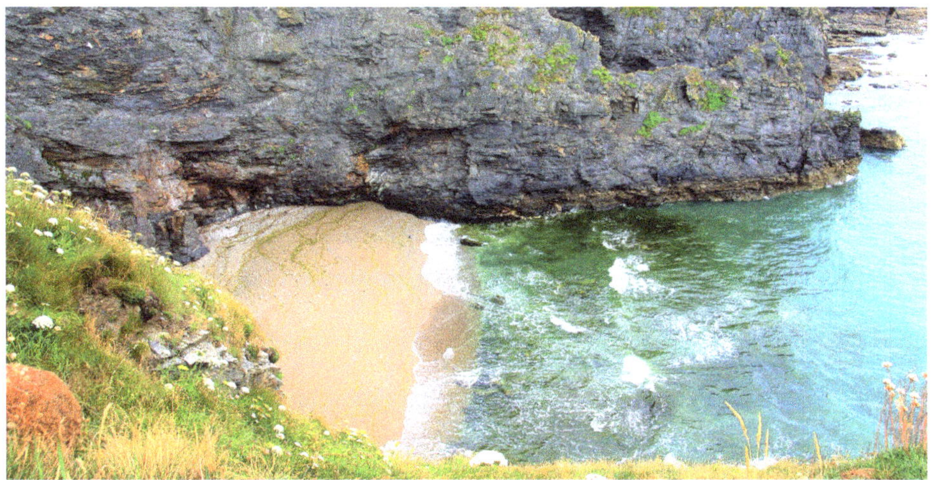
A little cove at Trewavas Head.

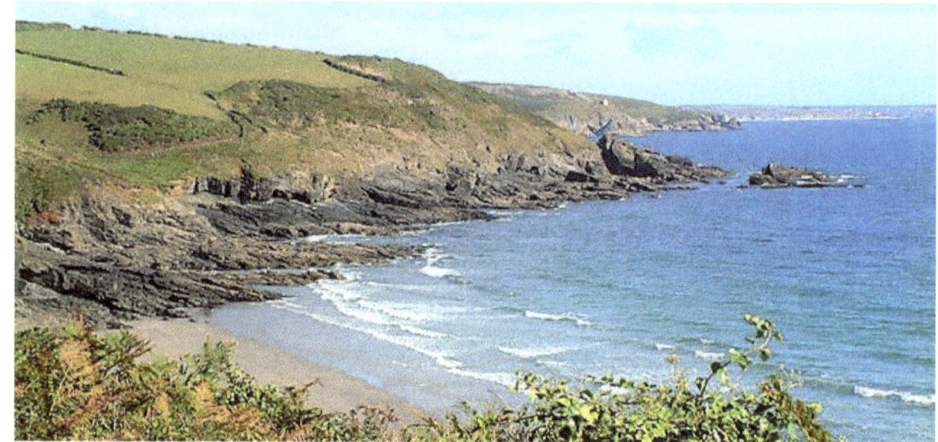

The stunning Kenneggy Sands.

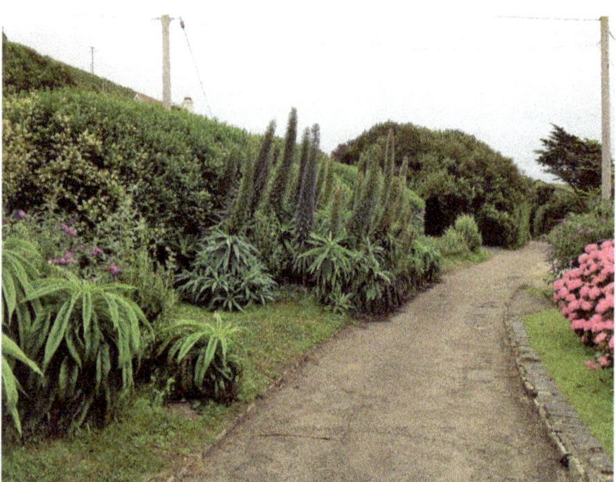

Tropical plants thrive in West Cornwall.

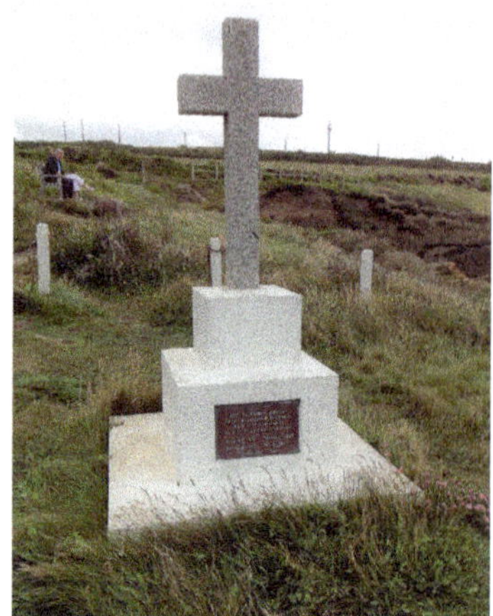

Memorial to 22 fishermen.

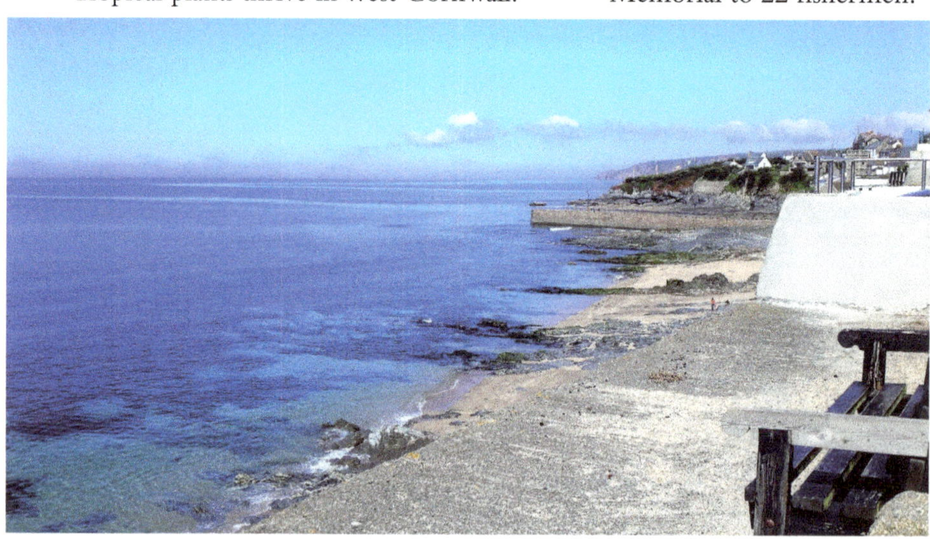

At Porthleven, looking back along the harbour and coast.

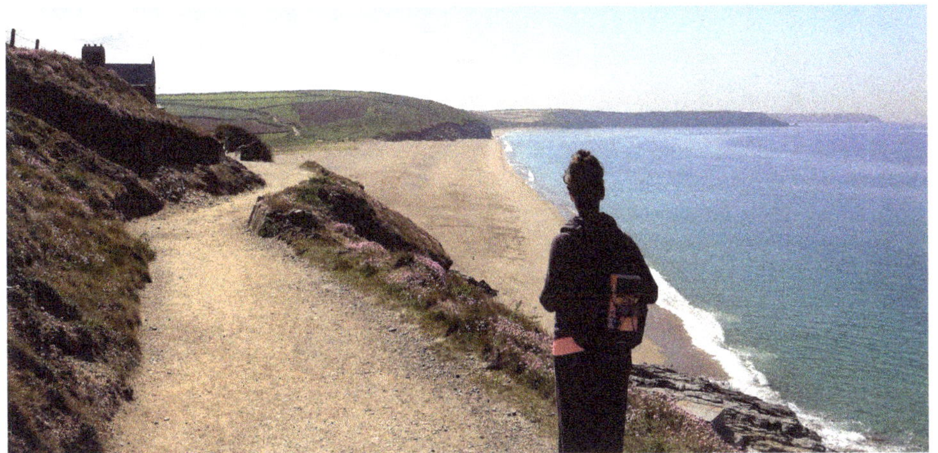

Looking across Porthleven Sands to The Lizard.

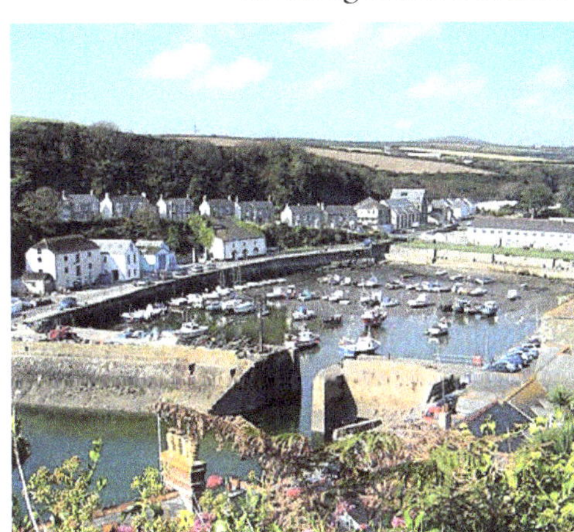

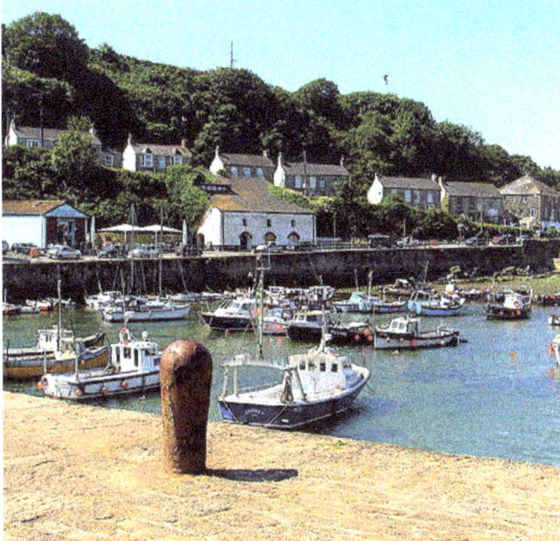

Porthleven Harbour.

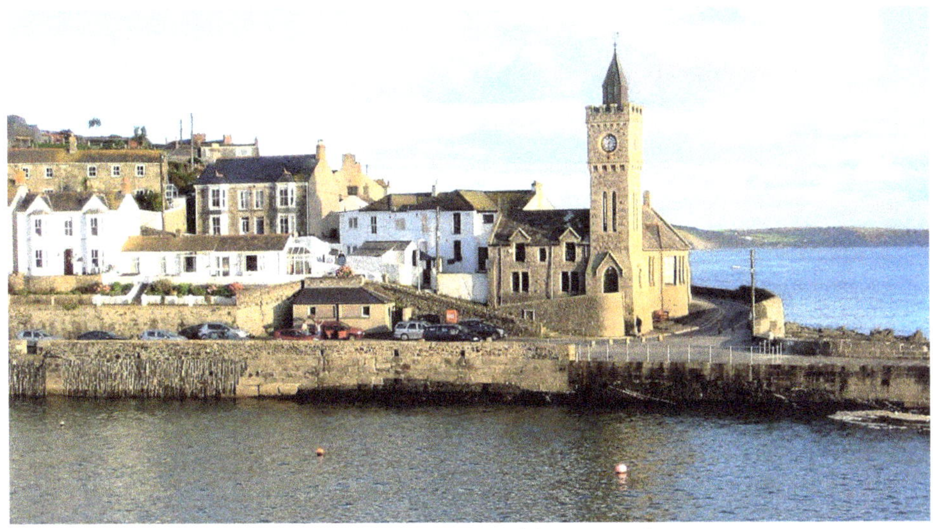

The Clock Tower at Porthleven Harbour.

Porthleven to Lizard Point

A beautiful section of the coastal path awaits you between Porthleven and The Lizard, with almost guaranteed solitude for most of the day if you decide to walk this section.

Leaving Porthleven, the coast runs straight for the next three miles along the golden beach of Porthleven Sands, half way along which is the impressive Loe Bar. In Cornish the word 'loe' means a pool of water, and the water which is trapped behind the beach (at Loe Bar) is the largest natural body of fresh water in the whole of Cornwall.

After passing by the impressive beach at Porthleven the coastline weaves its way in a southerly direction, with stunning little coves and beaches which include the delightful Poldhu Cove and Church Cove.

The small town of Mullion is soon reached which meets the sea at the picturesque Mullion Cove. Looking out from Mullion Cove to the ocean the large Mullion Island can be seen just off shore, which is home to a variety of sea birds that use the islands steep slopes to rear their chicks.

This really is a beautiful section of the coastal path, and one of the south west coast path's most romantic and awe-inspiring landmarks lies between Mullion and Lizard Point. This is the amazing Kynance Cove which is truly the jewel on the Lizard Peninsula. Its name derives from the old Cornish word kewnans which means 'ravine' and a stream makes its way through the adjacent valley down across the beach. If you find yourself down on the Lizard Peninsula then you must pay Kynance Cove a visit and soak up some of the beauty of this stunning area.

Lizard Point is the most southerly place in Britain and is a fantastic place. The lighthouse here as been in service since 1751 to protect any ships from the surrounding reefs which are deadly in this area. In the past this was often the welcoming beacon to travellers making their way back to the British Isles.

It is said by mariners that on a clear night, the light being emitted from the Lizard Point Lighthouse can be seen up to 100 miles away. Making this a sight for sore eyes for those weary and homesick explorers, that may have been at sea for many weeks.

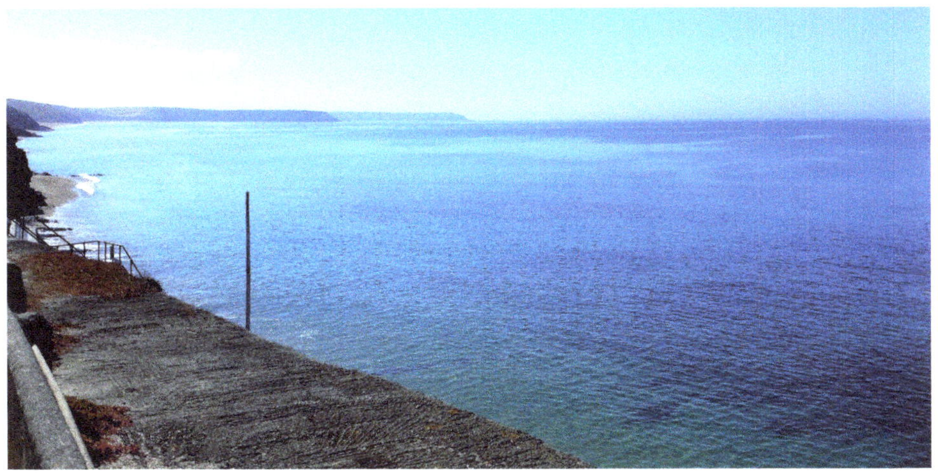
Looking south from Porthleven, along the coast towards Lizard Point.

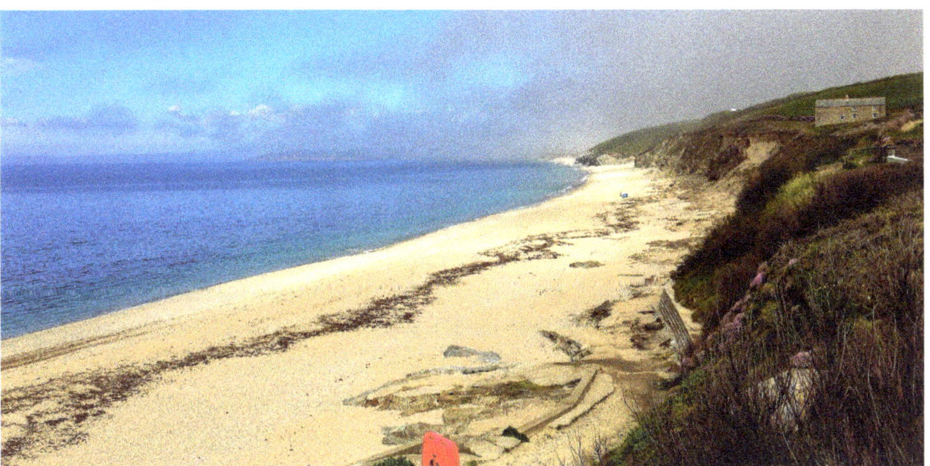
Golden beach at Porthleven Sands.

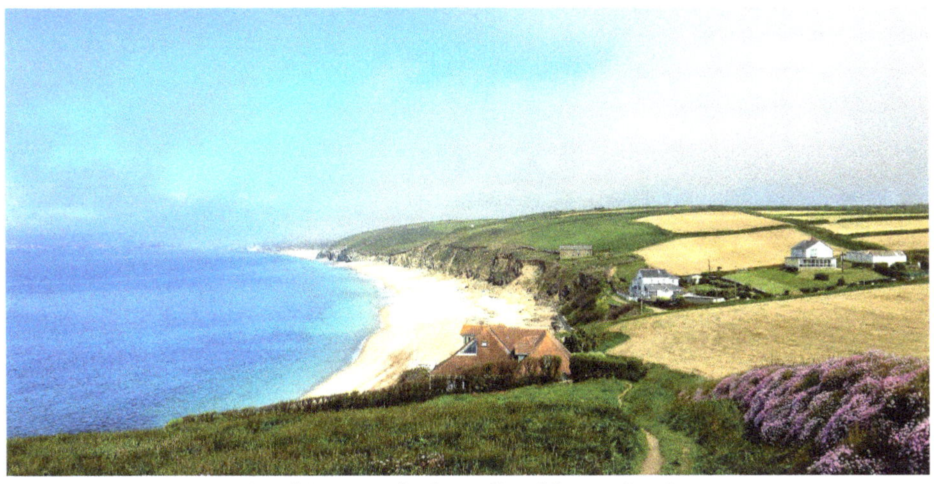
Looking north along Porthleven Sands.

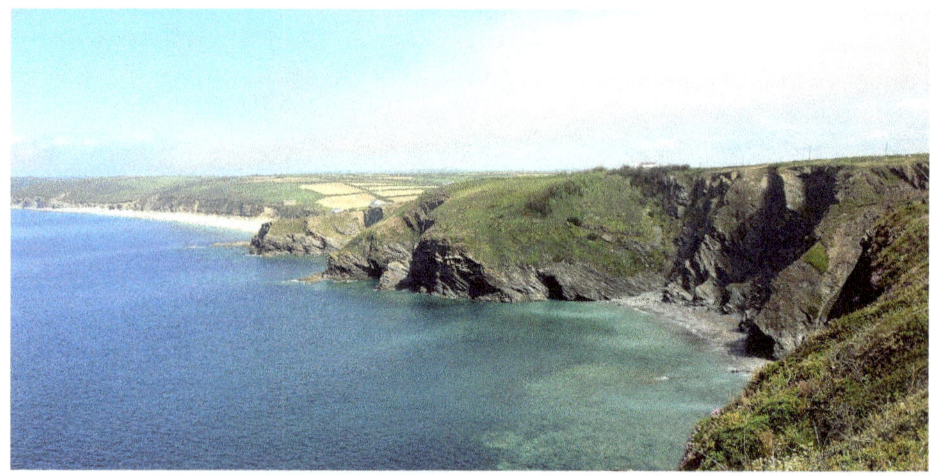
A remote and stunning coastline between Porthleven and Mullion Cove.

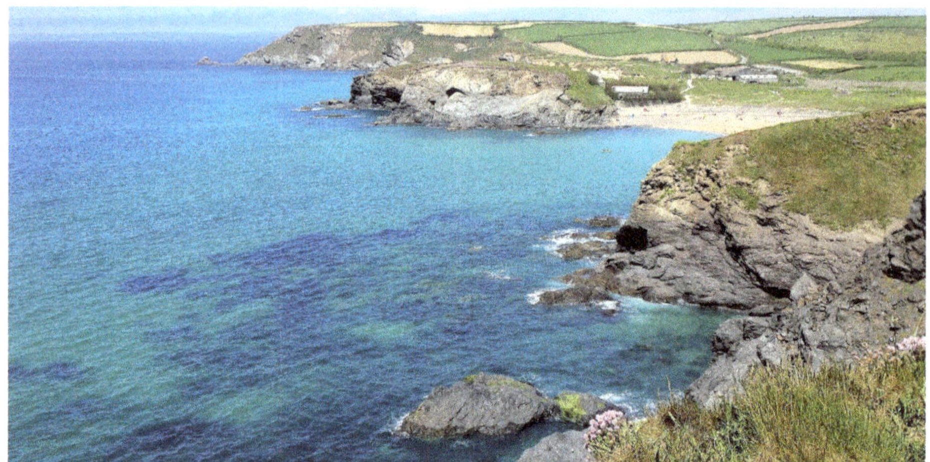
Looking north at Church Cove and the beautiful surrounding coastline.

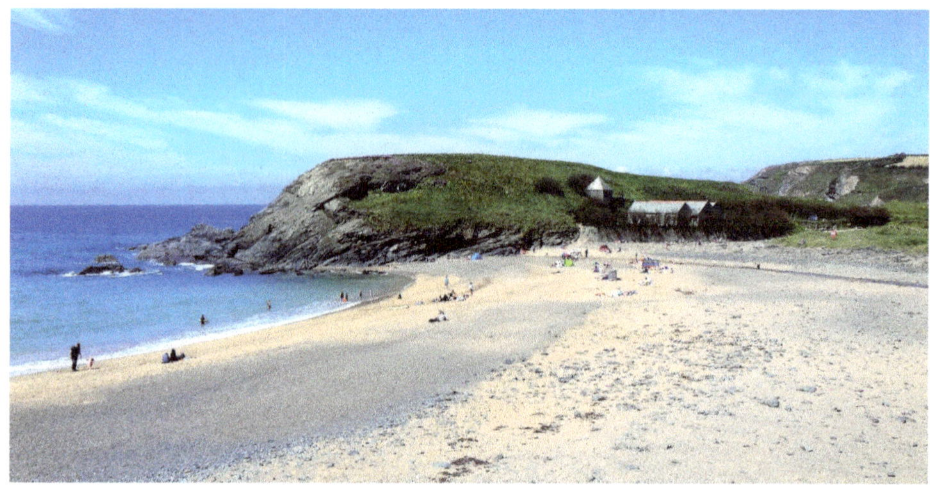
The beautiful setting of Church Cove.

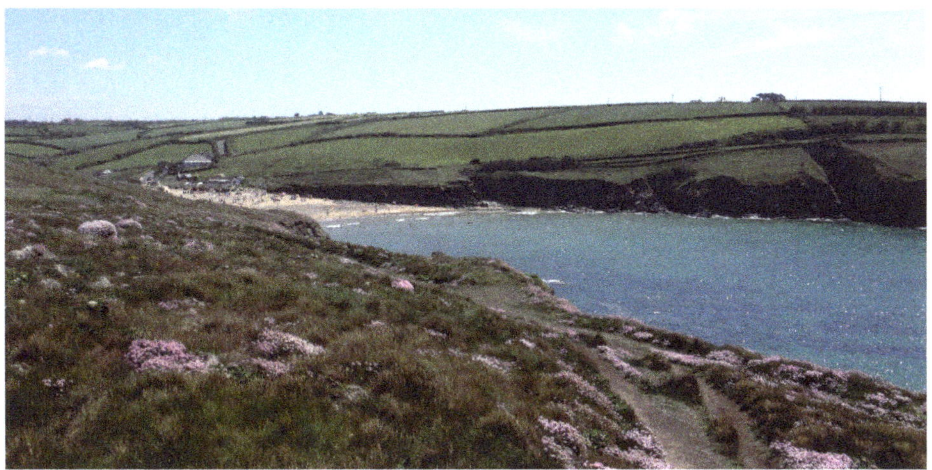
Approaching Poldhu Cove on the South West Coast Path.

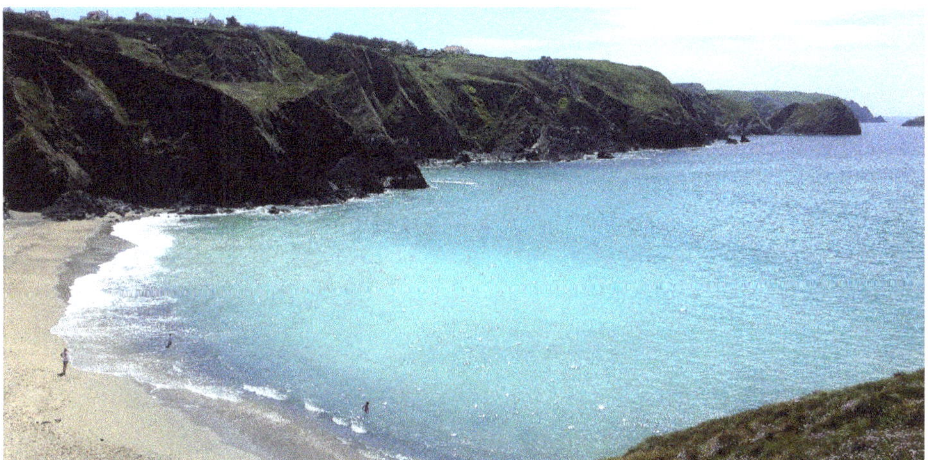
Poldhu Cove and its sandy beach.

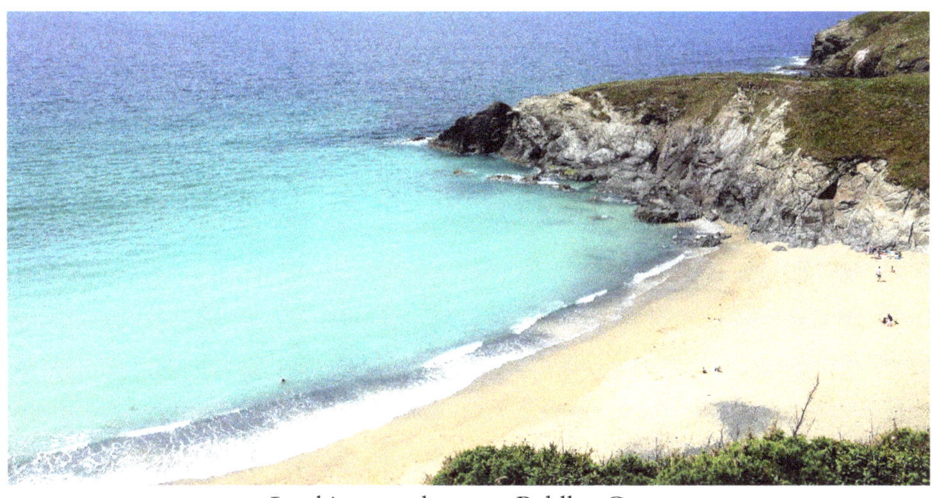
Looking north across Poldhu Cove.

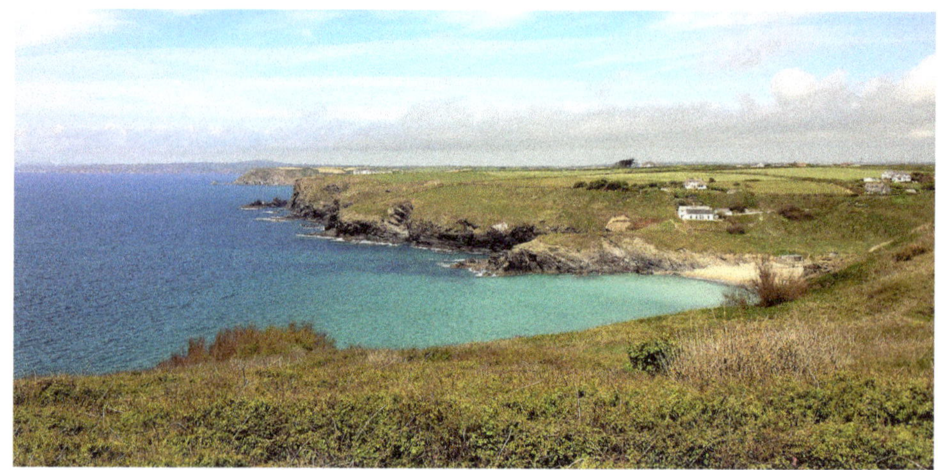

Beautiful coastline for as far as the eye can see.

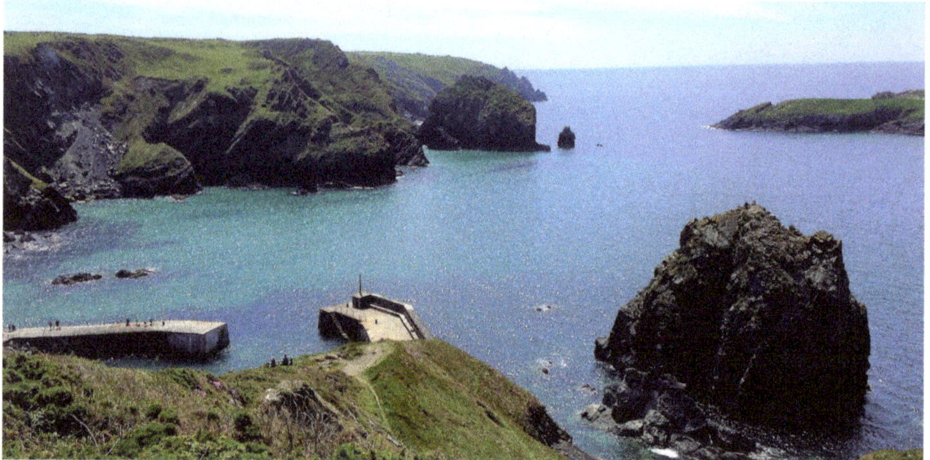

Mullion Cove and Harbour from the coast path. Mullion Island is top right.

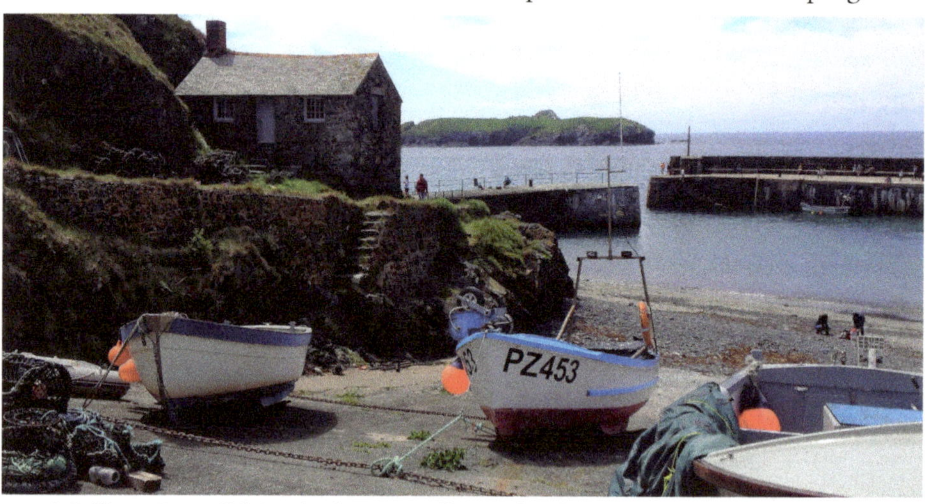

Mullion Cove fishing harbour. Mullion Island can be seen out in the bay.

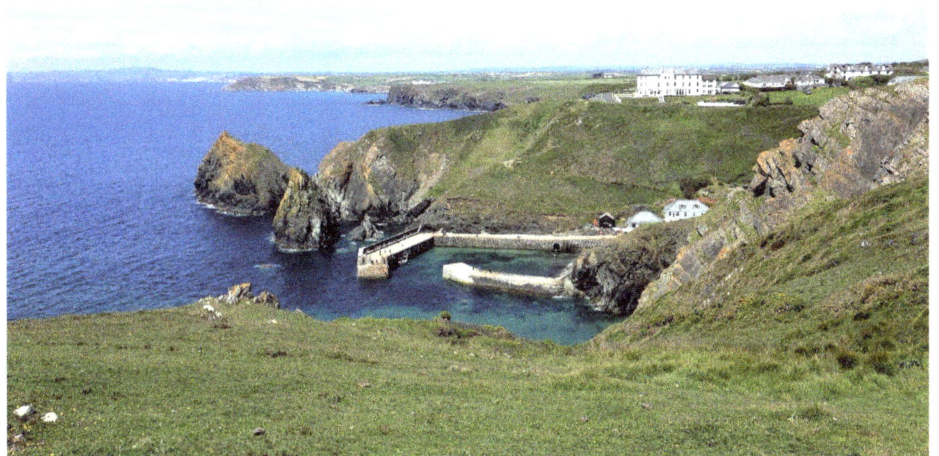

Looking down on Mullion Cove and its Harbour.

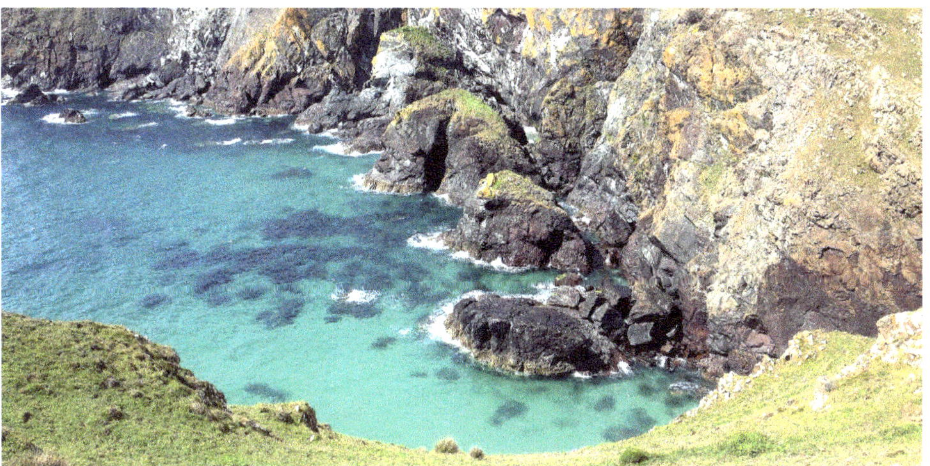

Crystal clear water surrounding the coastline.

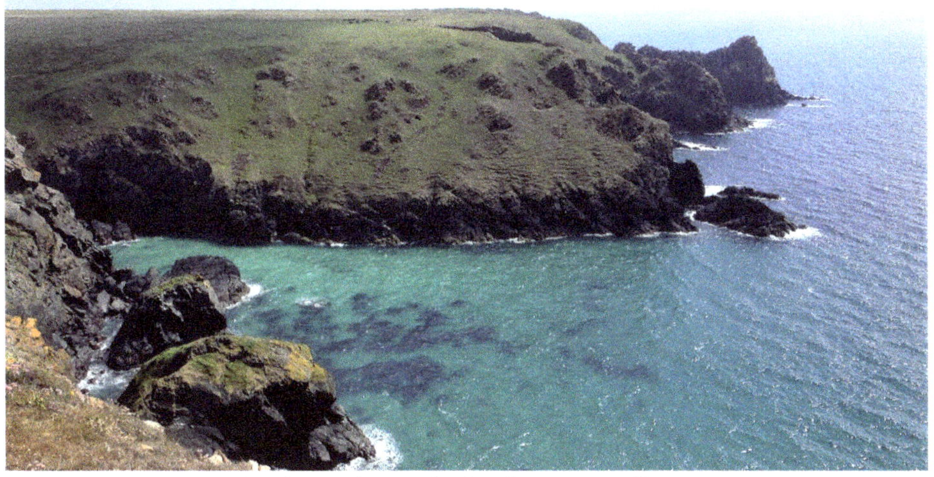

Near Predannack Head, after leaving Mullion Cove.

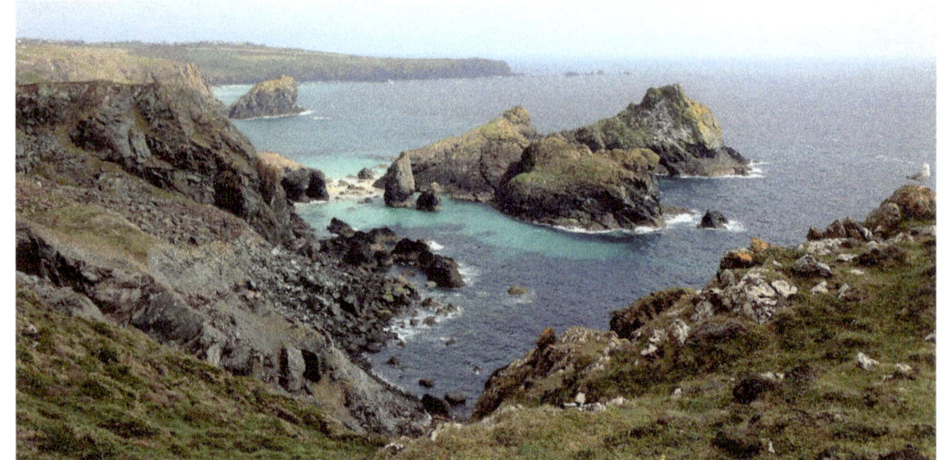

Above: Approaching the beautiful Kynance Cove. Below: Kynance Cove.

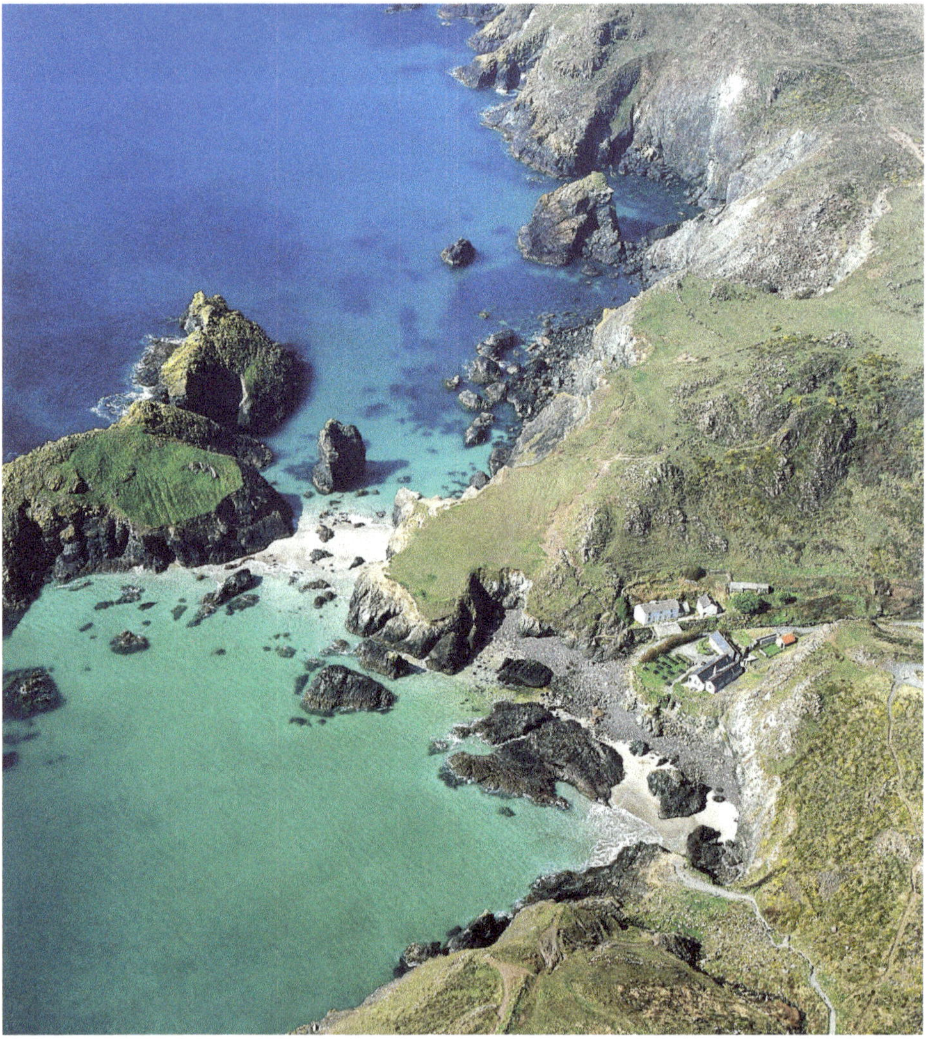

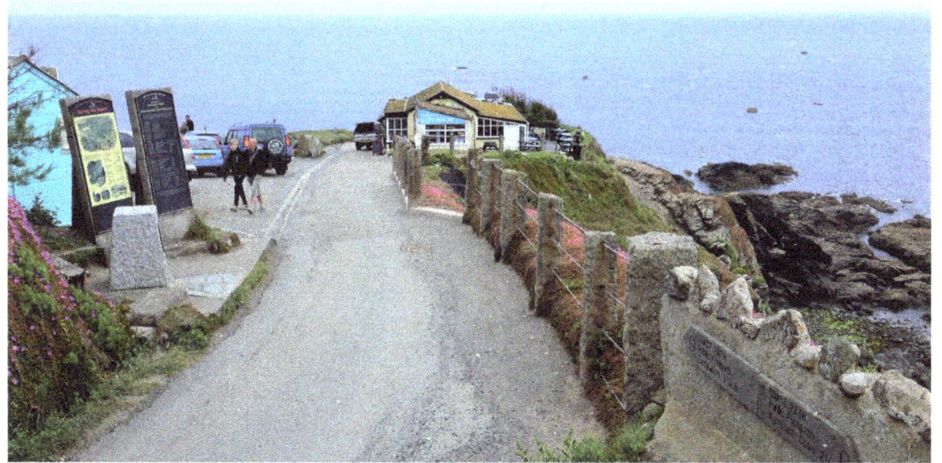
Dropping down the steep hill to Lizard Point.

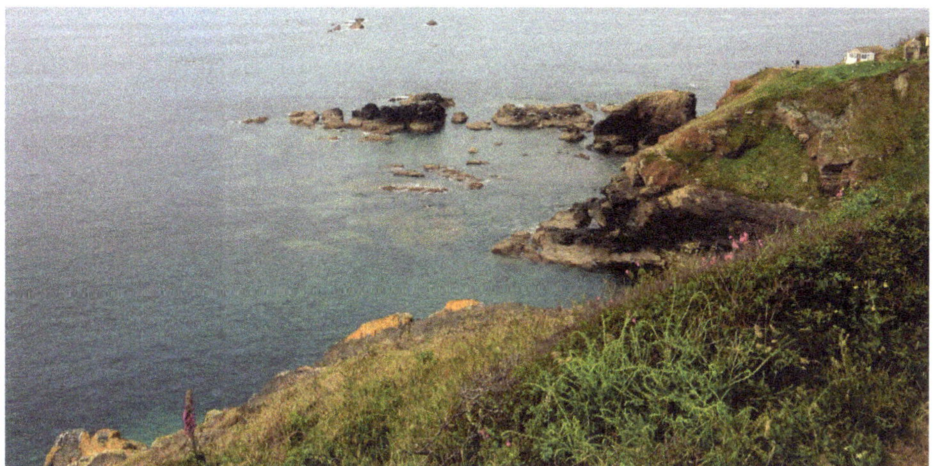
The dramatic setting of Lizard Point. The most southerly place in Britain.

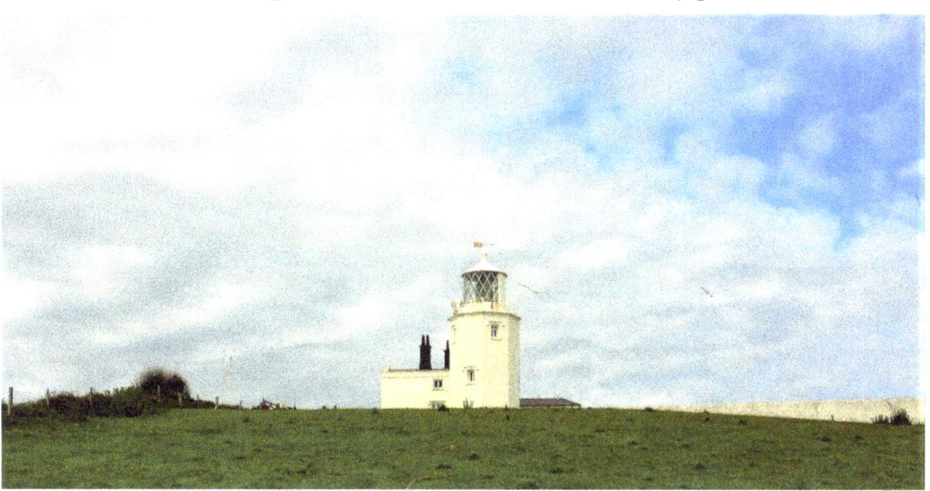
The majestic Lizard Point Lighthouse.

Lizard Point to St Keverne

This is a truly beautiful section of West Cornwall, and on this part of the coast lies the old fishing villages of Cadgwith and Coverack.

Cadgwith originally had the name 'Porthcaswydh' in old Cornish which meant 'a thicket', and this was due to the wooded valley surrounding the village. From the 16th century fishing has became the main occupation of the locals, and to this day fishing is still a huge part of this small community.

Just a few miles north of Cadgwith is the coastal village and fishing port of Coverack. This is a lovely village which not only has some wonderful pubs and restaurants, but also has a fishing harbour and a nice beach which is popular with the local windsurfers.

The coastline is exceptional here, and a relaxing day spent down in the coves and secluded beaches on this section of coast will leave you feeling invigorated.

St Keverne is an old village which lies just inland from the pretty beach at Godrevy Cove. It has a very peaceful and laid back atmosphere, which is in vast contrast to some of the events which took place in this small village's history. Back in 1497 the local blacksmith Michael An Gof led the first Cornish rebellion, which actually started in the village. A monument still stands proud to commemorate this famous local, whose leadership took the rebel army right to the edge of London where they were unfortunately defeated at the Battle of Deptford Bridge.

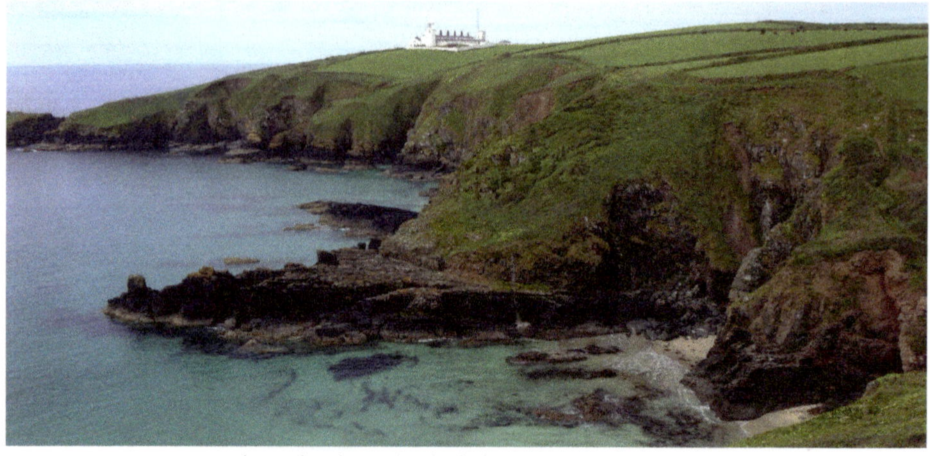

Looking back at the lighthouse on Lizard Point.

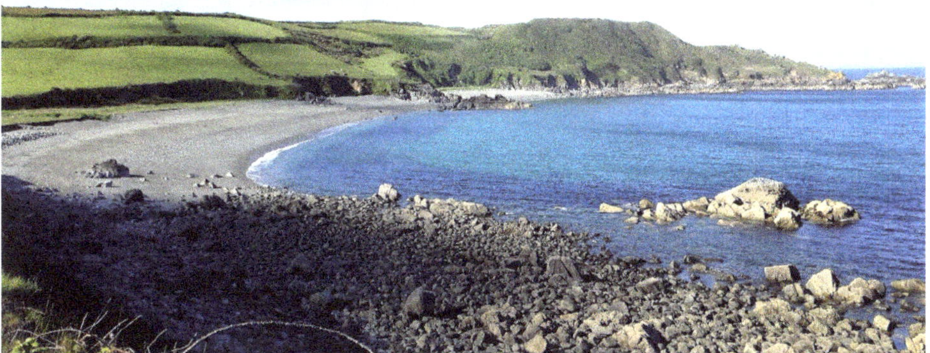

Godrevy Bay: the beauty of this section of the Cornish coastline is evident.

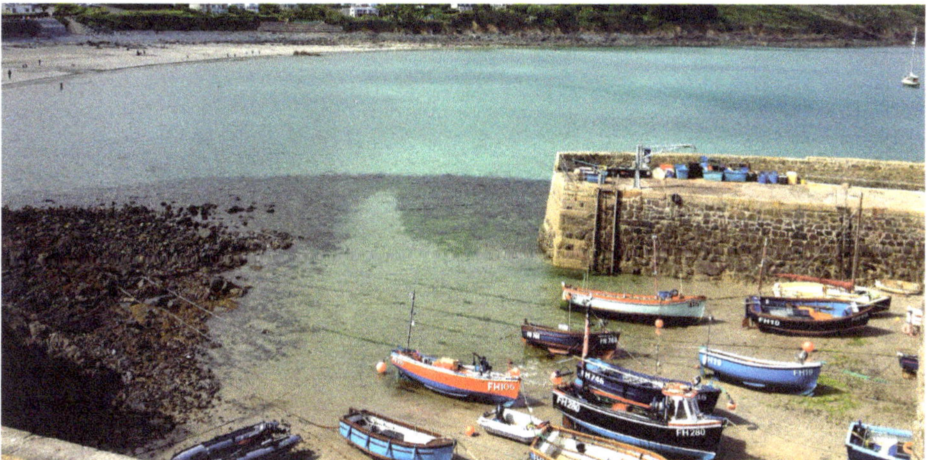

Looking across Coverack's Bay, from the harbour at Dolor Point.

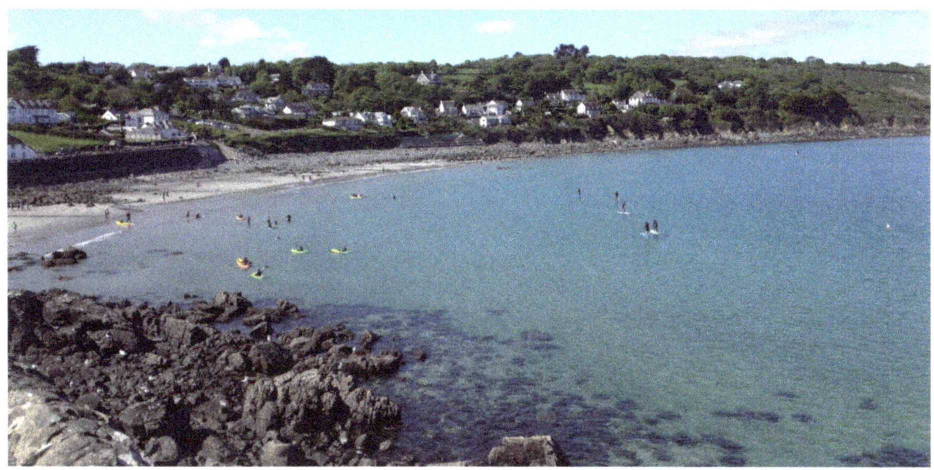

The stunning fishing village of Coverack.

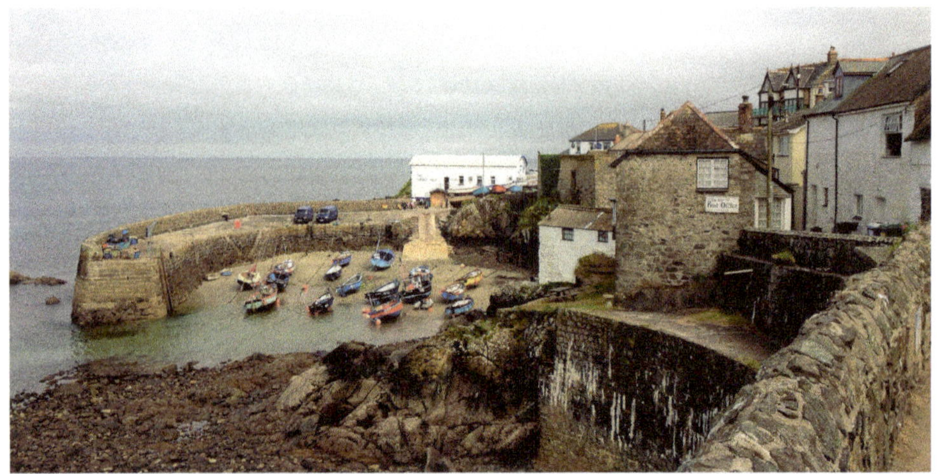
Coverack's pretty harbour with fishing boats moored within it.

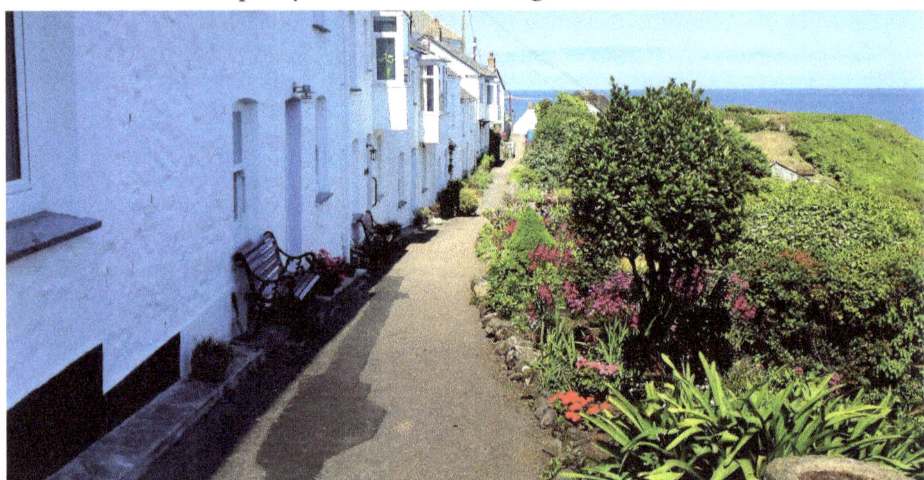
The picturesque Coverack and some of its old cottages.

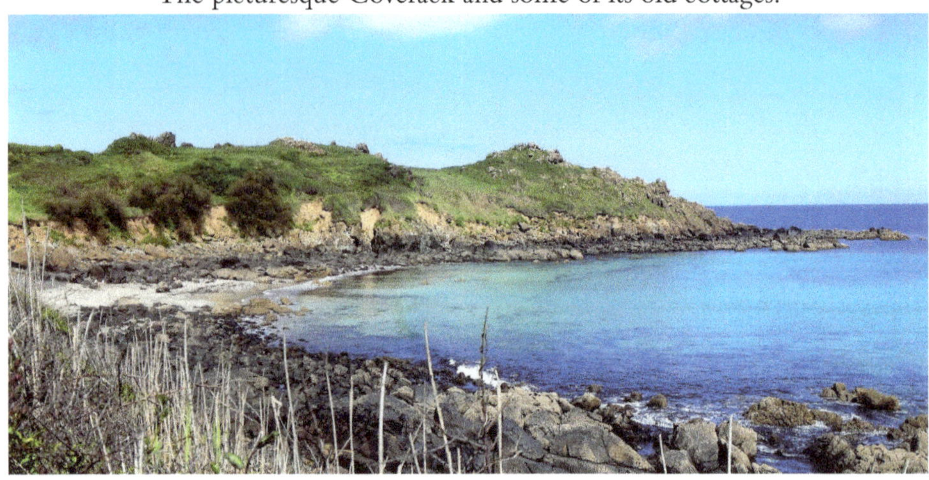
This is a very scenic and secluded coastline.

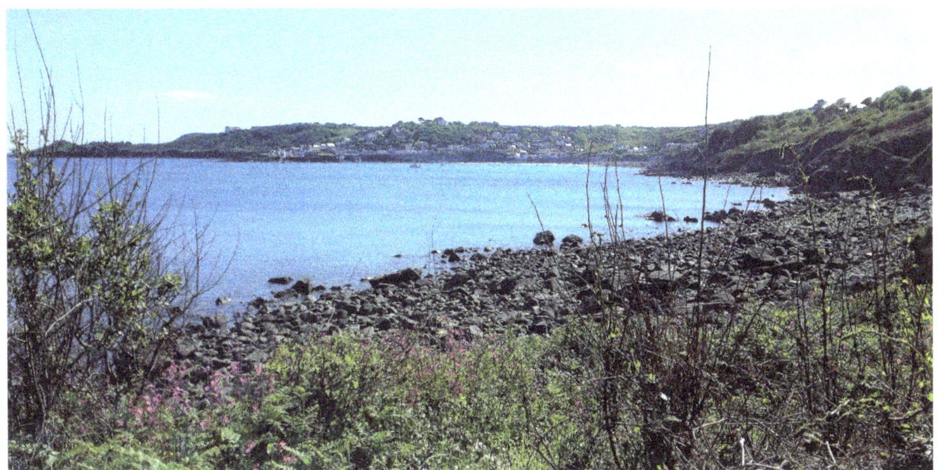

Looking back towards Coverack.

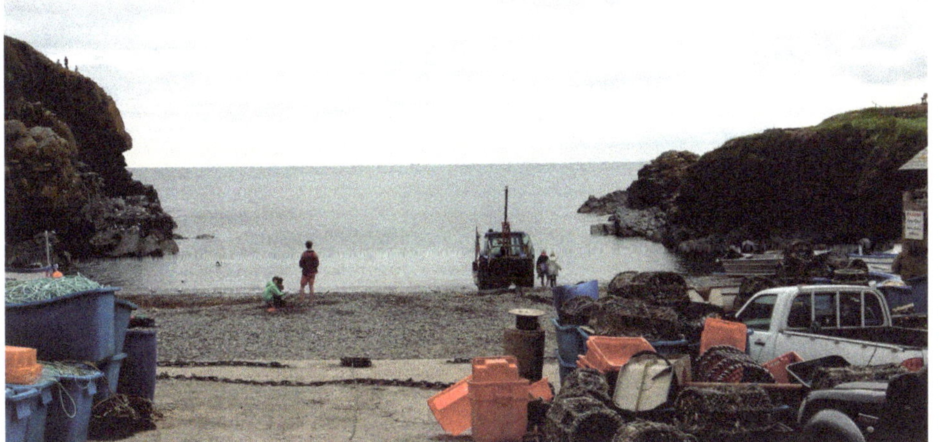

The lovely little cove and harbour at Cadgwith.

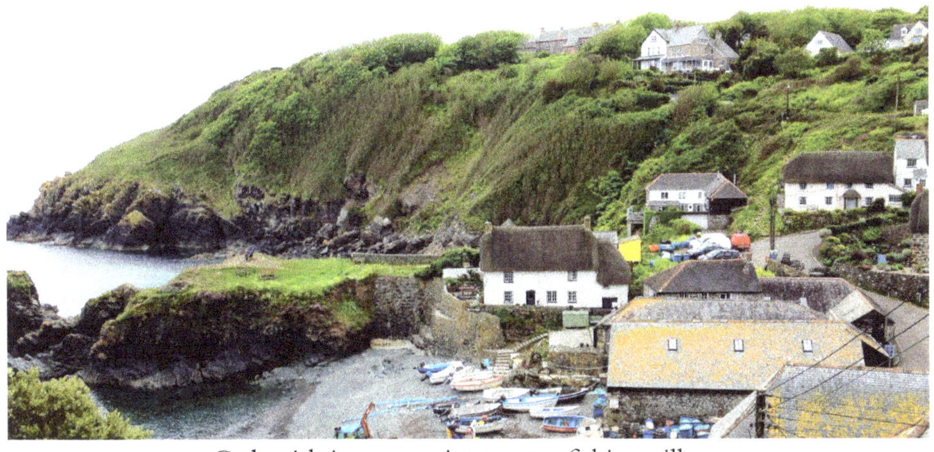

Cadgwith is a very picturesque fishing village.

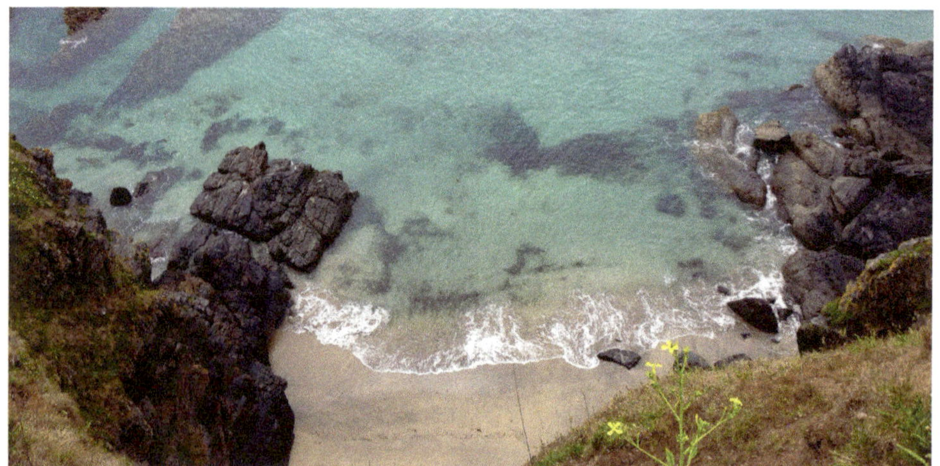

Beautiful coves and crystal clear, turquoise sea surrounding The Lizard.

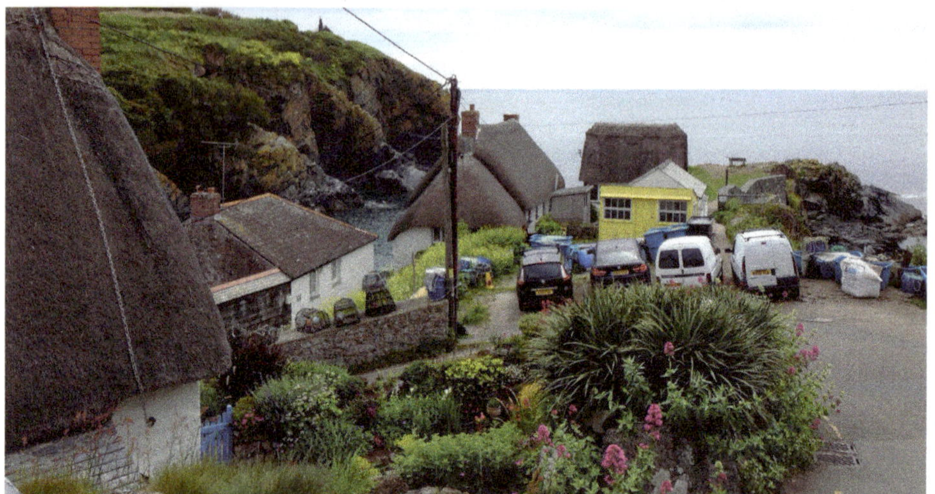

Walking into Cadgwith, with its pretty thatched cottages all around.

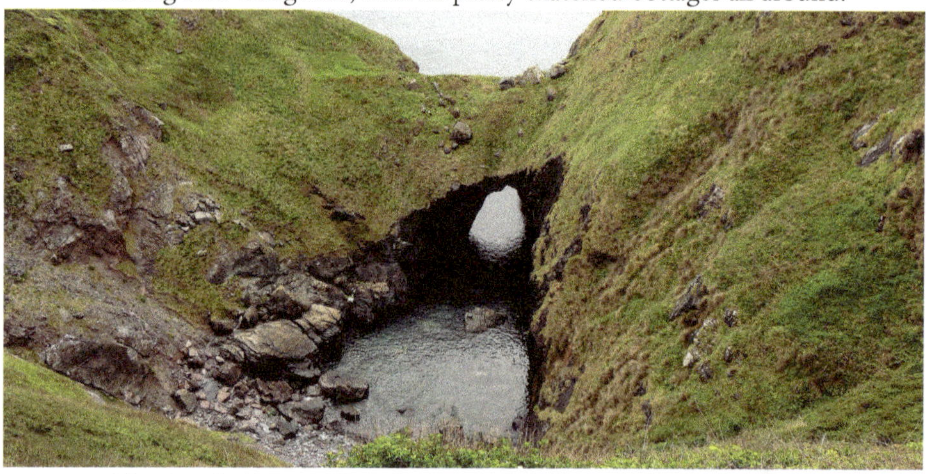

The Devils Frying Pan which is just to the south of Cadgwith.

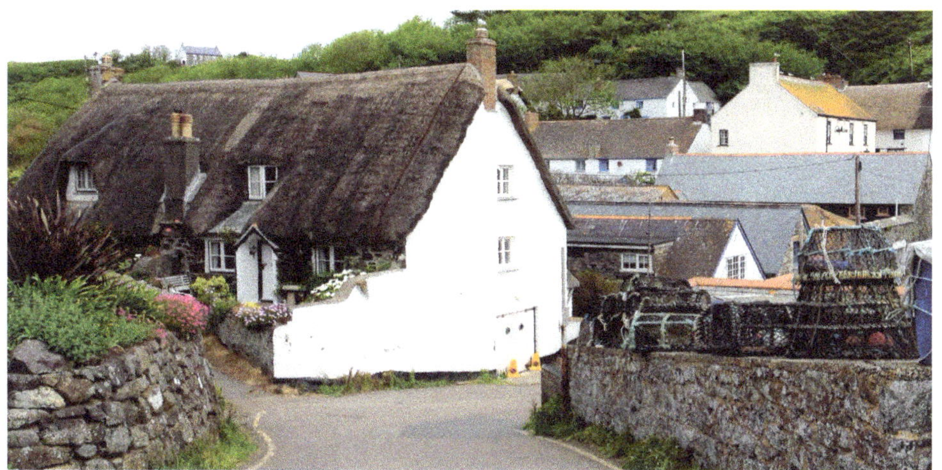
Traditional thatched cottages and lobster pots at Cadgwith.

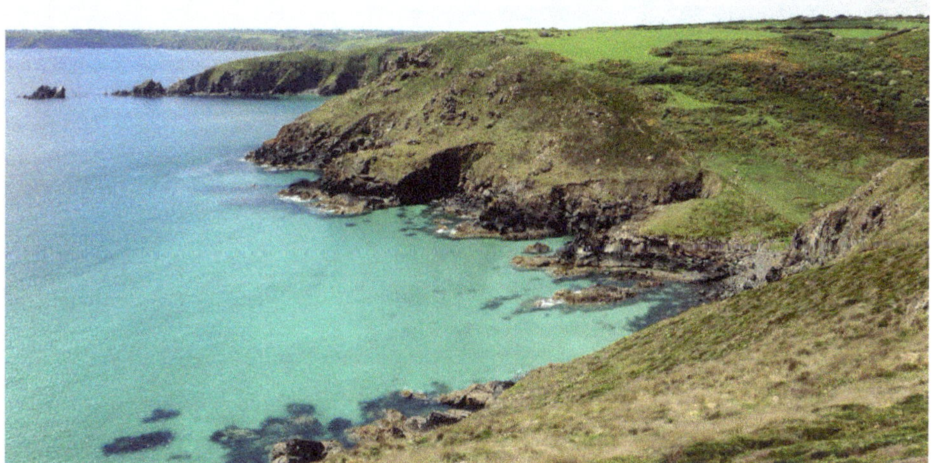
Above and below: The stunning coastline between Cadgwith and Coverack.

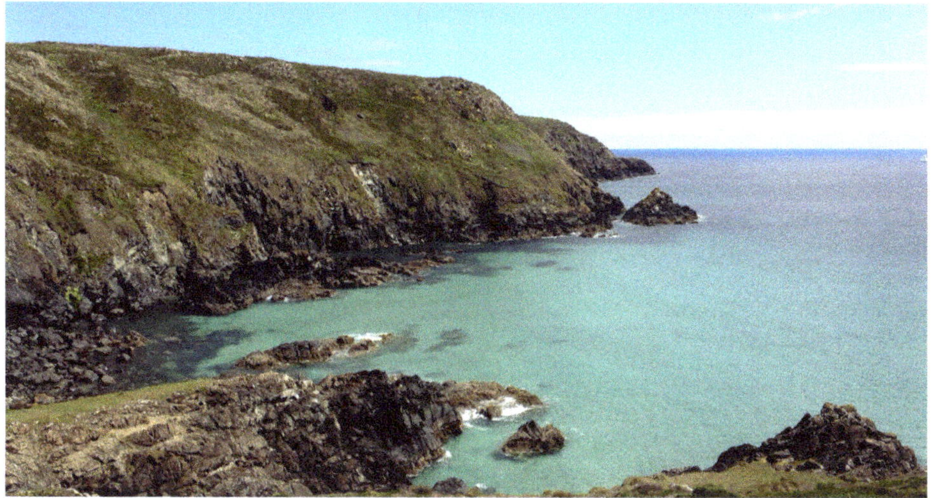

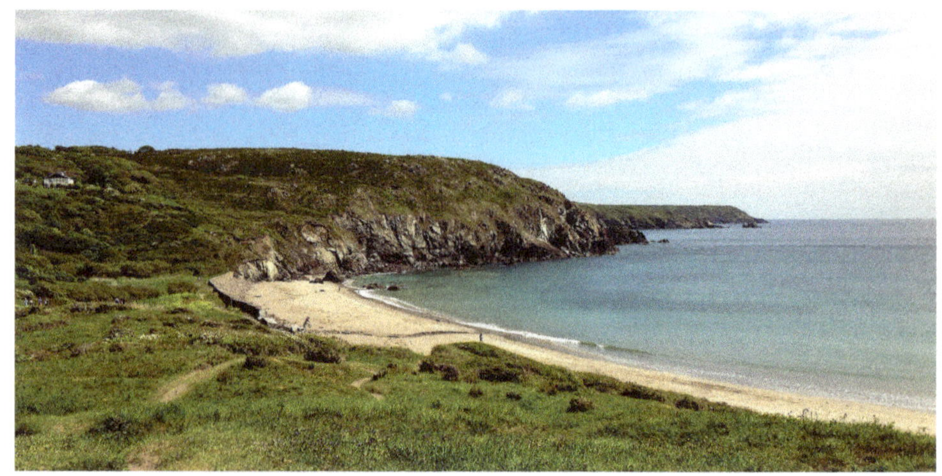

Kennack Sands, between Cadgwith and Black Head.

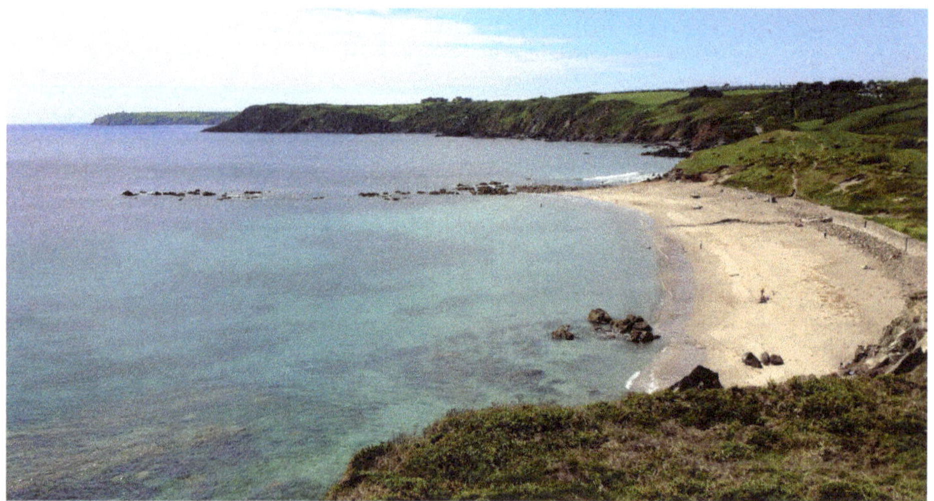

Looking south across the coastline and Kennack Sands.

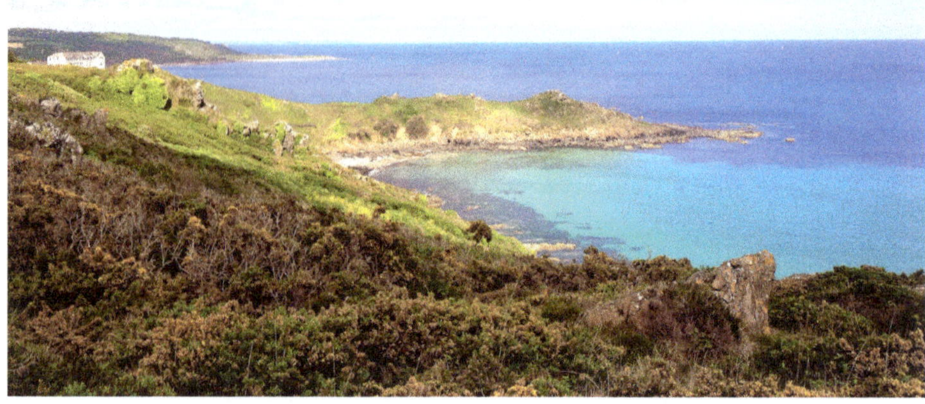

The beautiful Chynhalls Point, just south of Coverack.

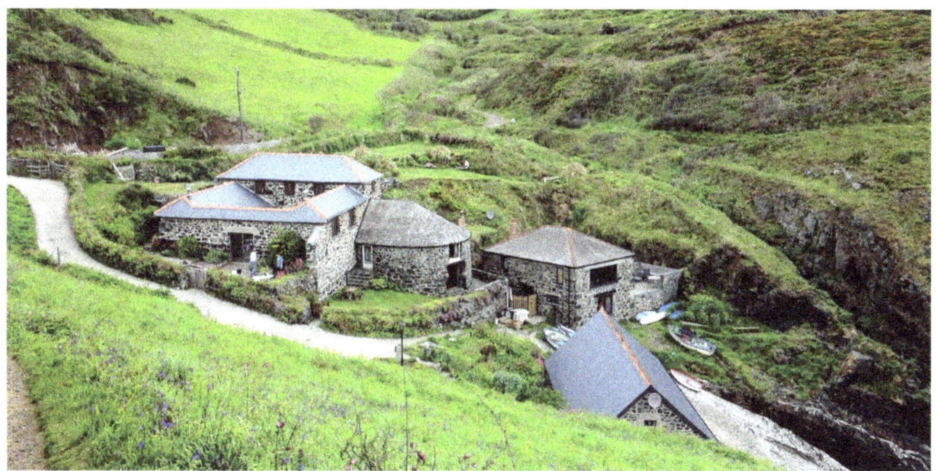
After Lizard Point - the beautiful setting of Church Cove.

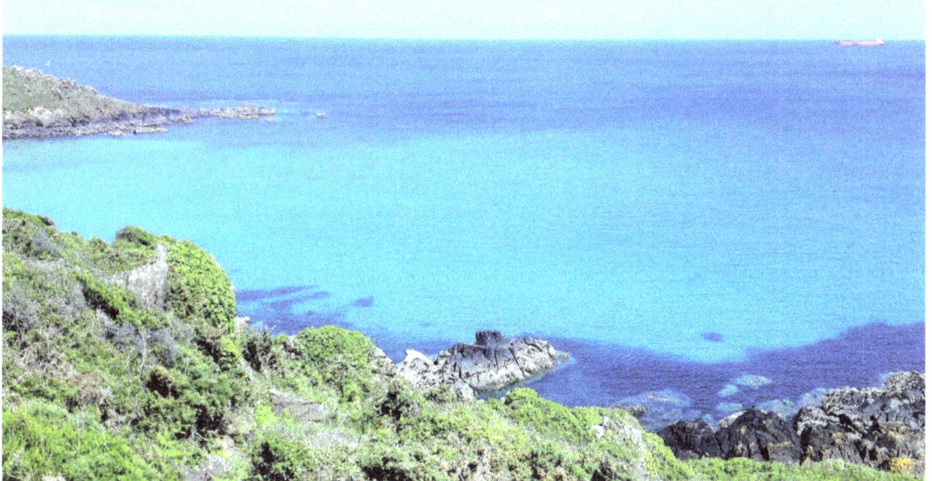
Looking out to the Atlantic Ocean on a calm day near St Keverne.

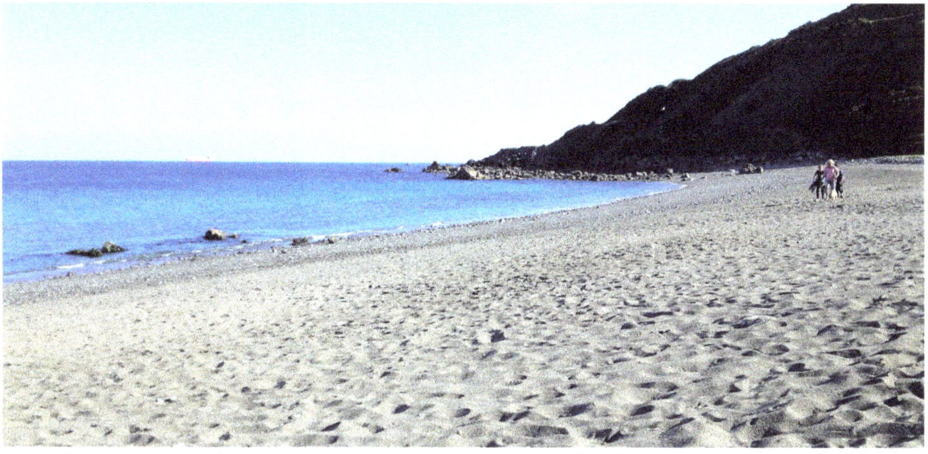
The pretty Godrevy Cove, St Keverne is just inland from this lovely beach.

St Keverne to Helford

The remnants of large scale quarrying took place just north of St Keverne, where the popular 'serpentine rock' was mined and exported via ships from the area. This fabulous looking stone can often look like the skin of a lizard, which is how this beautiful peninsula inherited its name.

If you are walking on the south west coast path then you will have to take a diversion inland at this point to bypass the disused quarries which hug the coastline. The coast path rejoins the ocean at Porthallow which is a little hamlet with a harbour.

After Porthallow the coastline turns at Nare Point and heads in a westerly direction towards the tiny hamlet of Gillan. In old Cornish the word 'gilenn' means nook or creek, and this is likely to be how this settlement got its name, as adjacent to the hamlet is Gillan Creek.

Around the next headland at Dennis Head you will be presented with the beautiful vista of the Helford River, which can now be followed until the coastline reached the delightful village of Helford. The Helford is one of the most unspoilt rivers in Cornwall and is absolutely stunning. The banks are lined with old oak trees and people can often be seen sailing up and down its crystal clear water.

Helford village is a real gem and you would be hard pushed to find a more attractive village anywhere in the British Isles. With old thatched cottages and pretty gardens which are bursting with colour during the summer months, the village is also flanked by the ever constant beauty of the Helford River and the lush foliage of the surrounding woodlands.

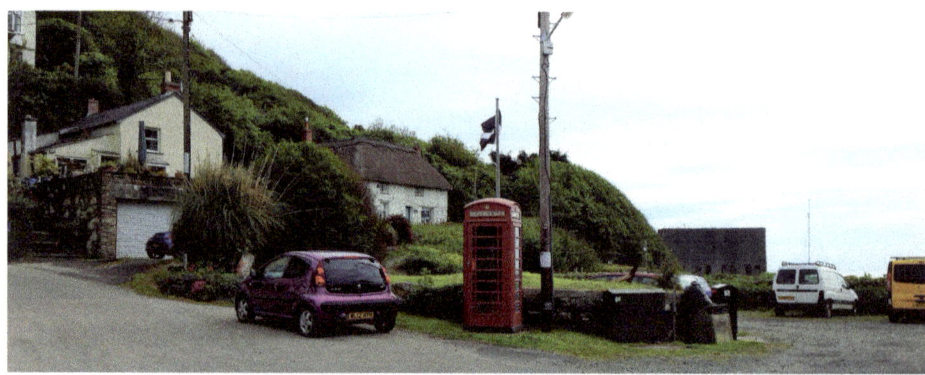

Near the harbour, at the tiny hamlet of Porthallow.

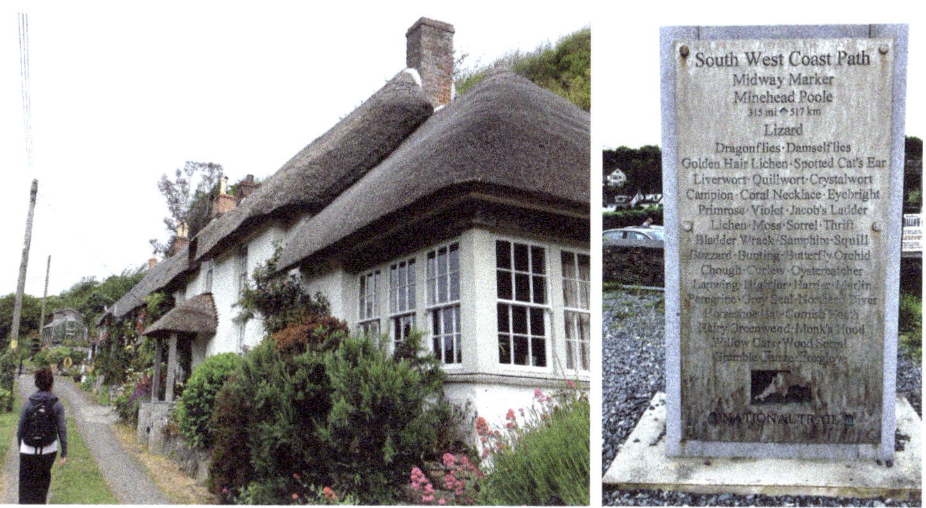

Beautiful cottages at Porthallow. Right, the SWCP half way marker at Porthallow.

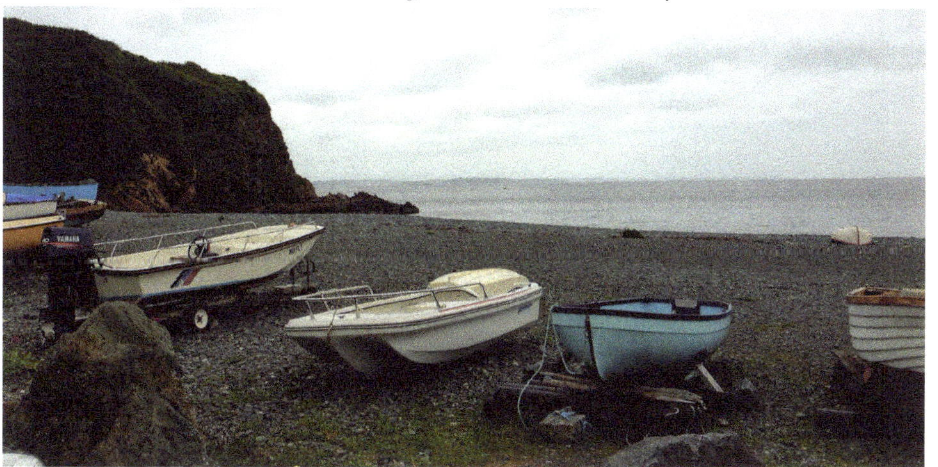

Boats sat on the pebble beach at Porthallow.

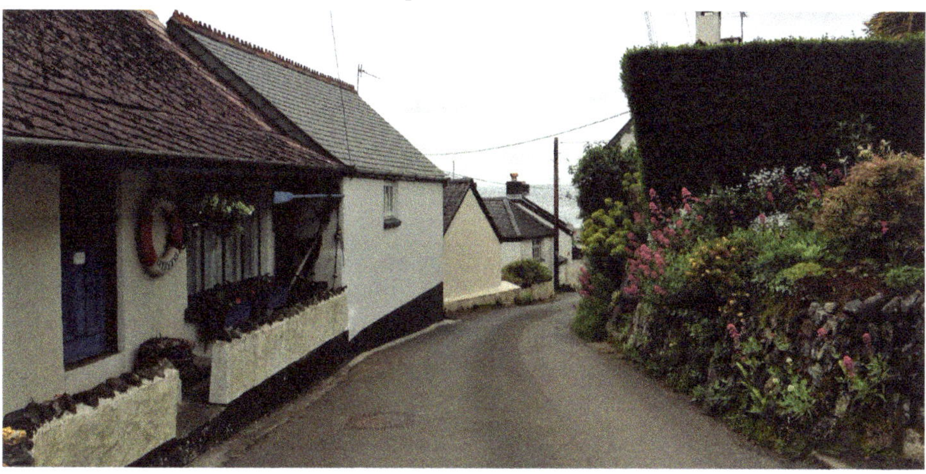

Near the top of the hill at the pretty hamlet of Porthallow.

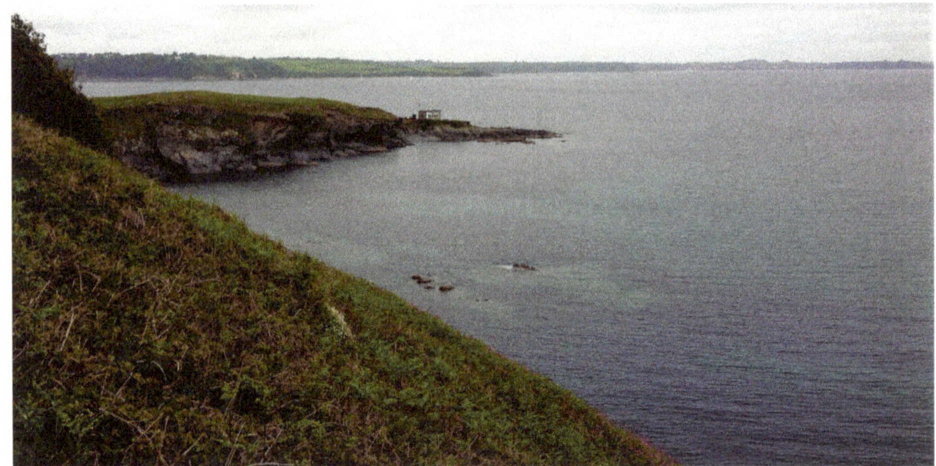
The 'coastwatch' look out station at Nare Point, near the hamlet of Gillan.

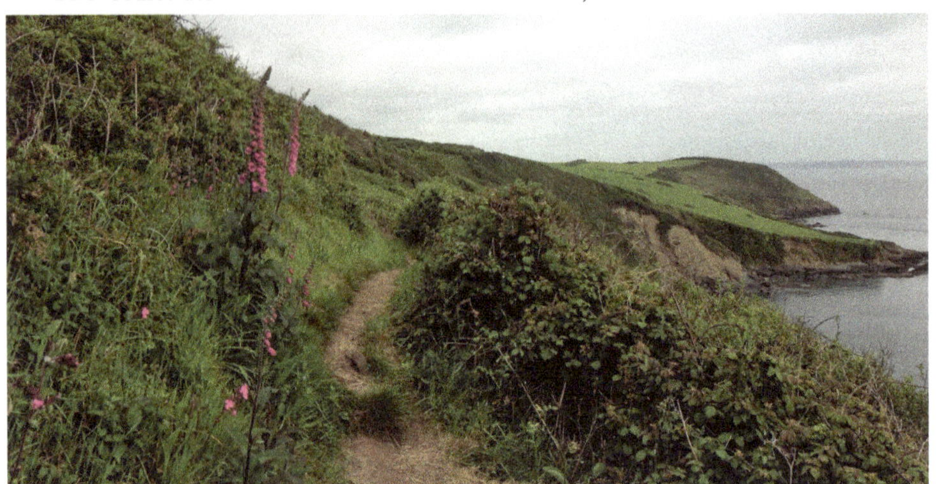
The coastal path nearing Gillan.

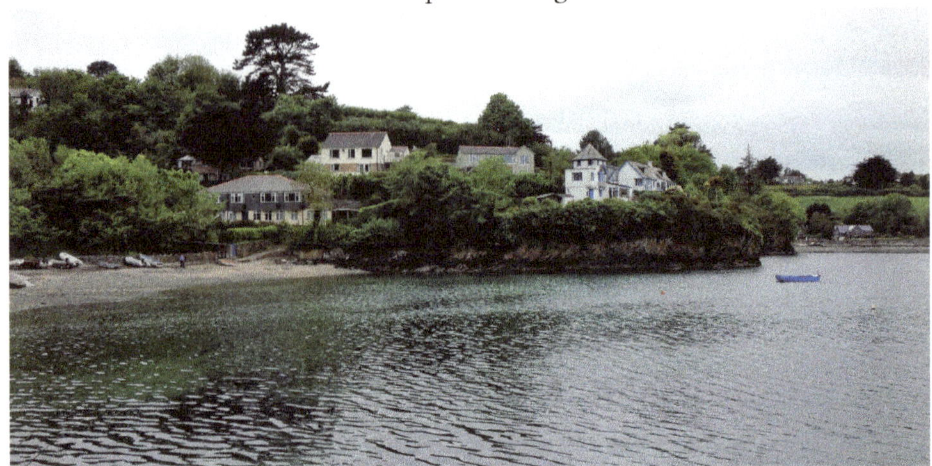
The picturesque and tranquil setting of Gillan.

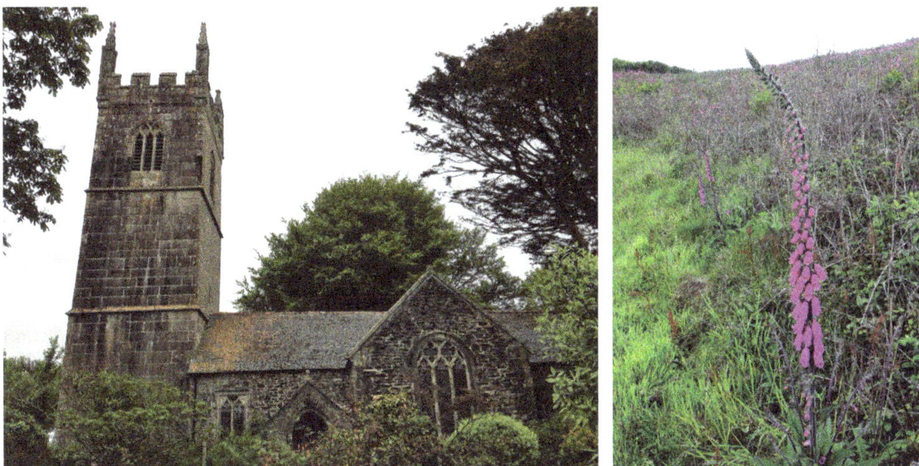

The parish church at St Anthony-in-Meneage, near the hamlet of Gillan.

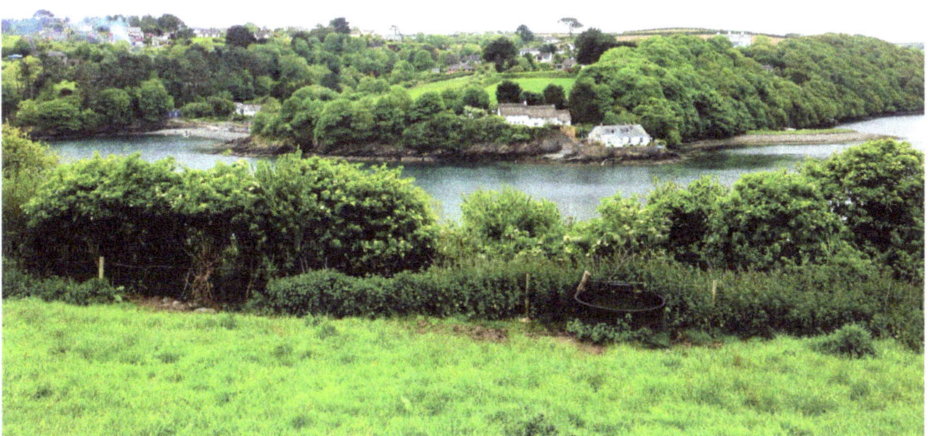

Looking across the Helford River to the beautiful Gillan Harbour.

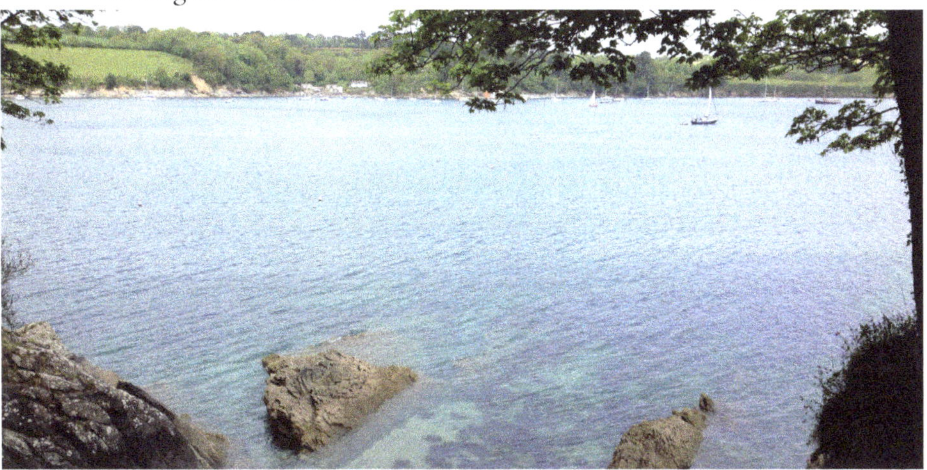

Yachts sailing on the stunning Helford River.

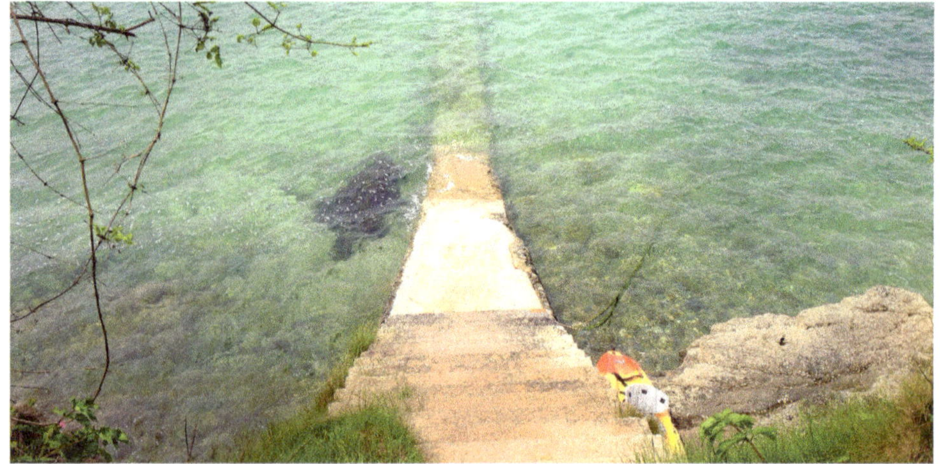

The water at Helford is completely clear and translucent.

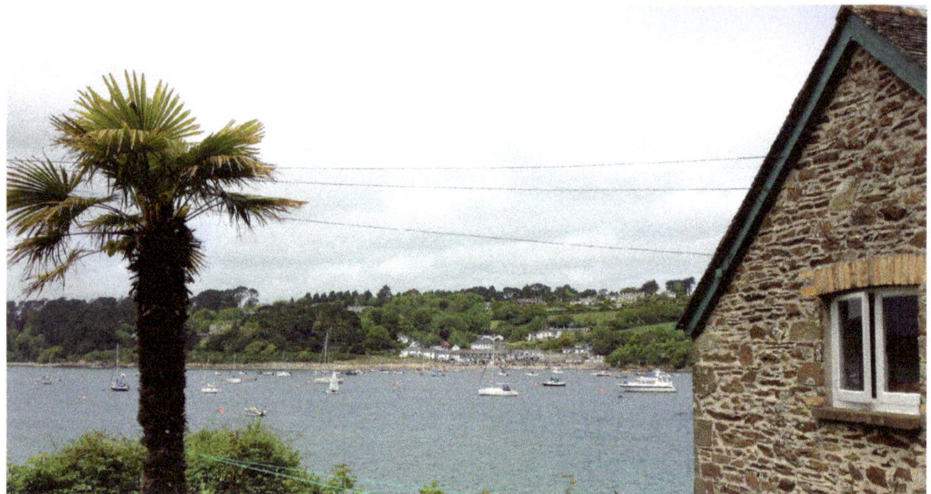

On the outskirts of Helford looking across the river.

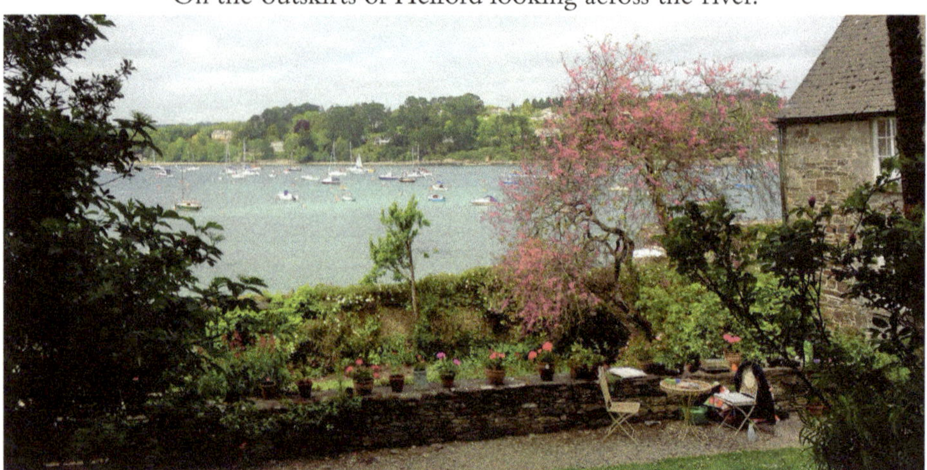

Beautiful scenes across the Helford River from this old cottage.

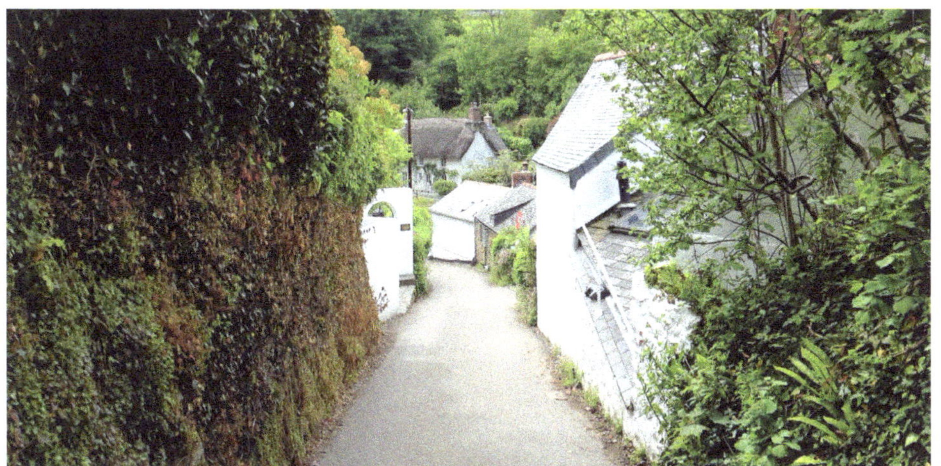

Old lanes and streets through the village of Helford.

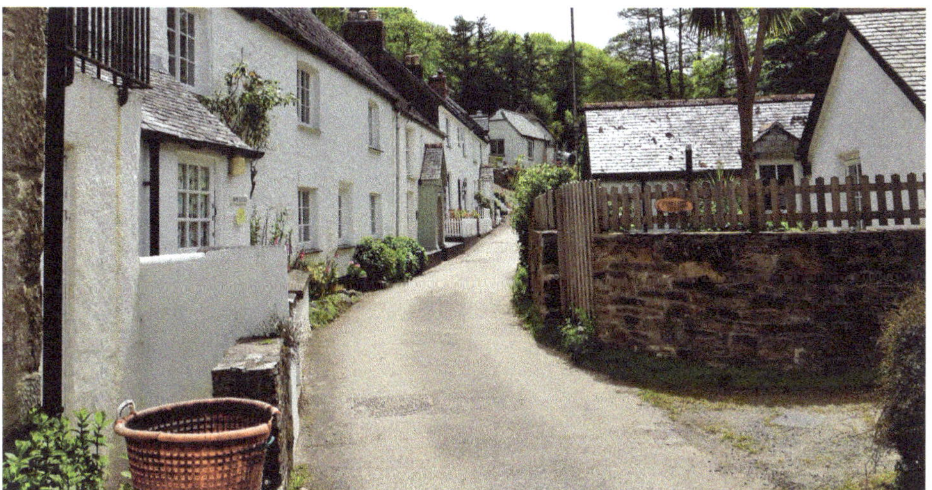

The village is littered with beautiful old cottages.

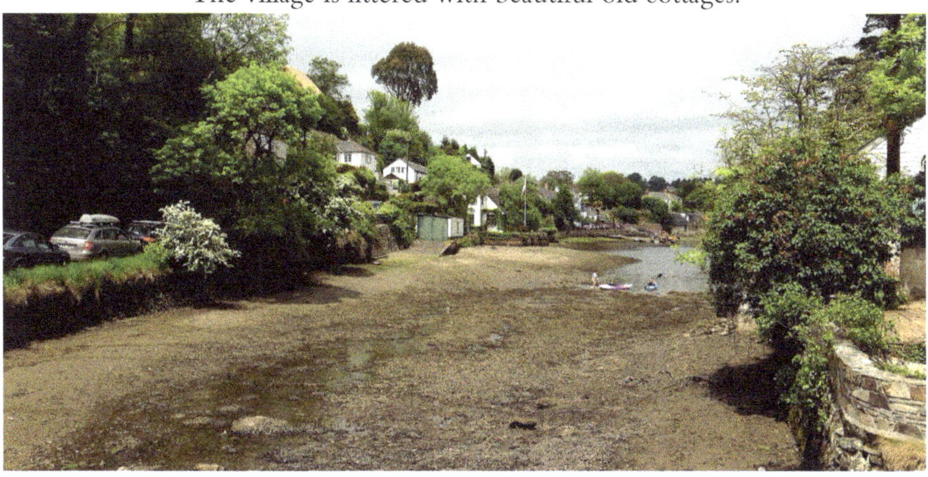

Looking along a creek at low tide in Helford.

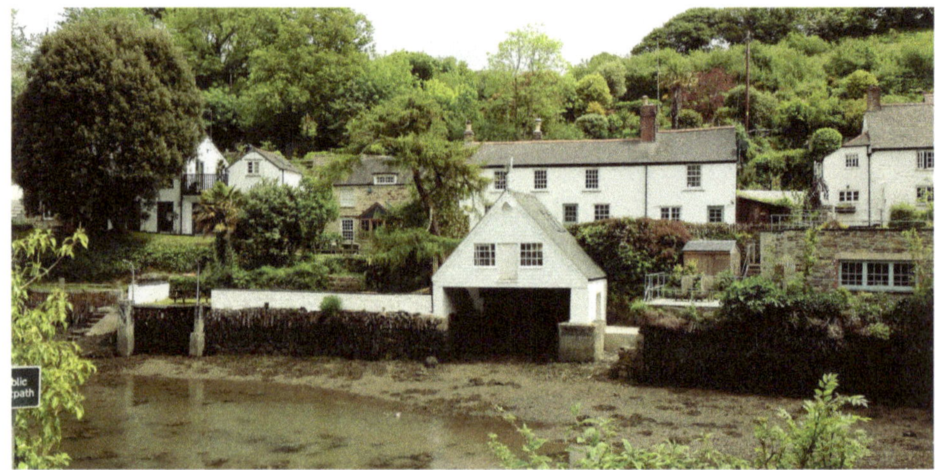

An attractive boat house in the heart of Helford village.

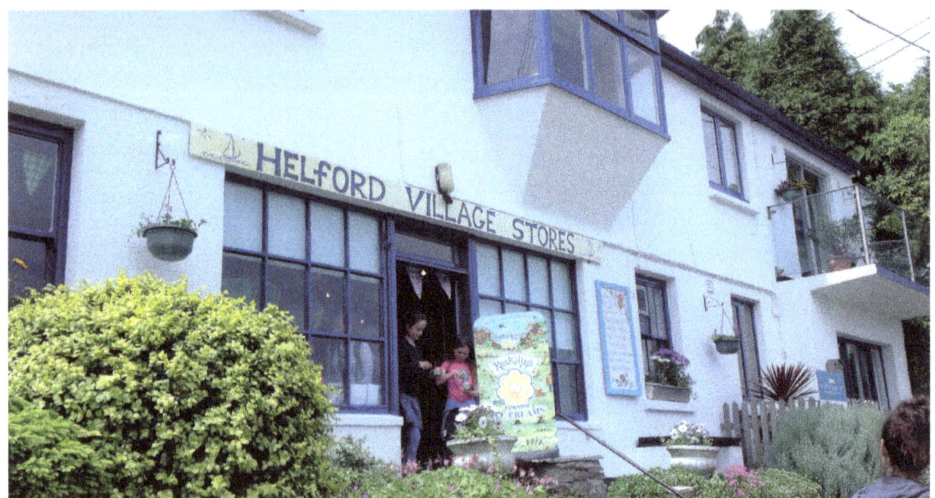

Helford village stores.

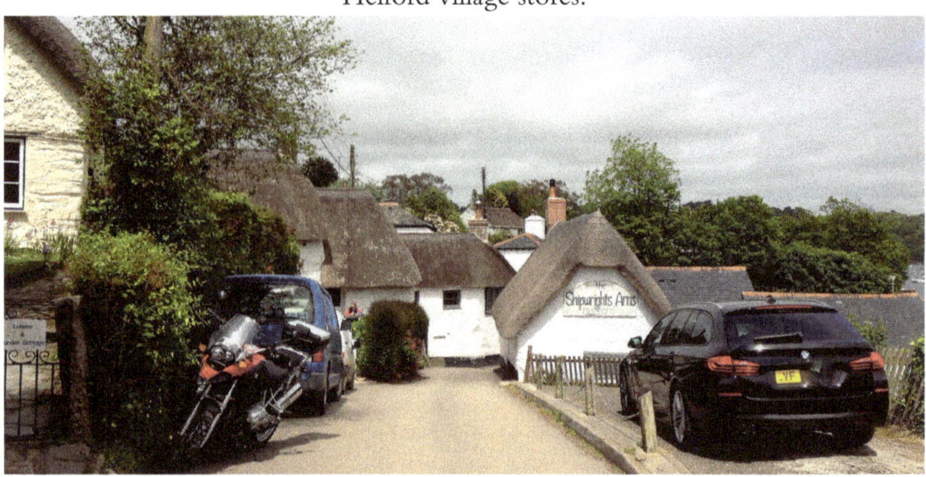

The Shipwrights Arms pub, with its lovely thatched roof.

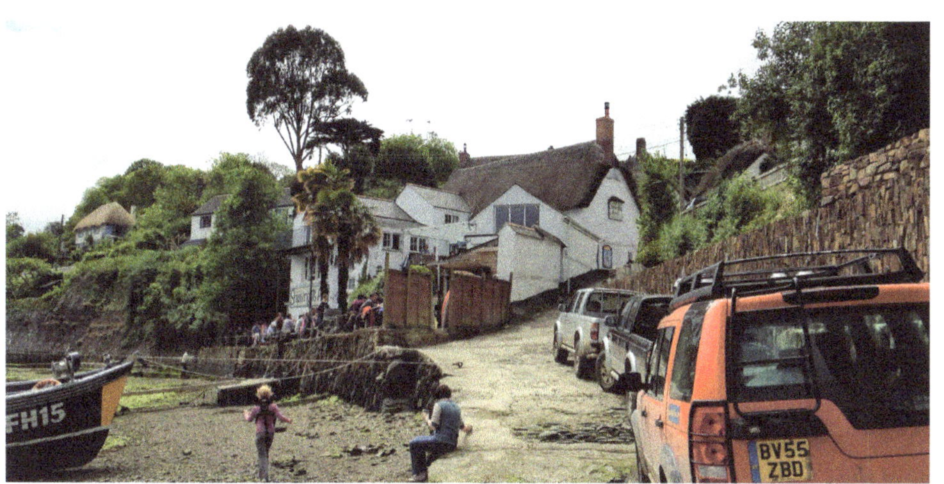

Looking up from the river towards The Shipwrights Arms.

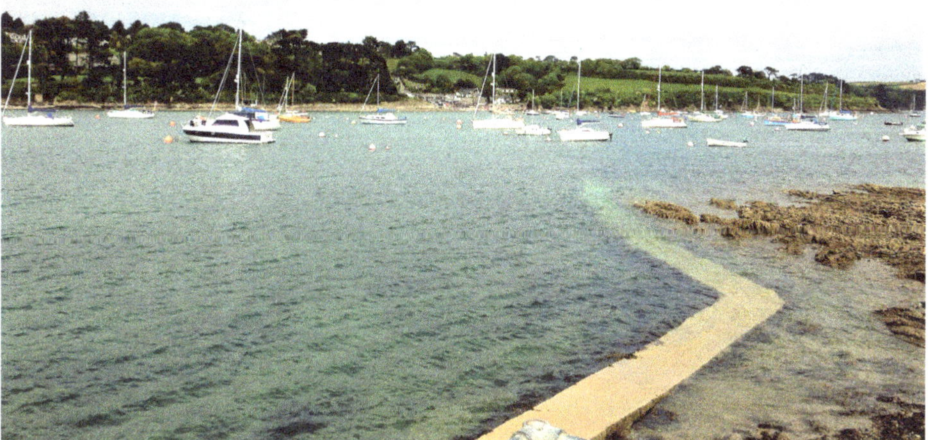
Yachts and fishing boats afloat on the Helford River.

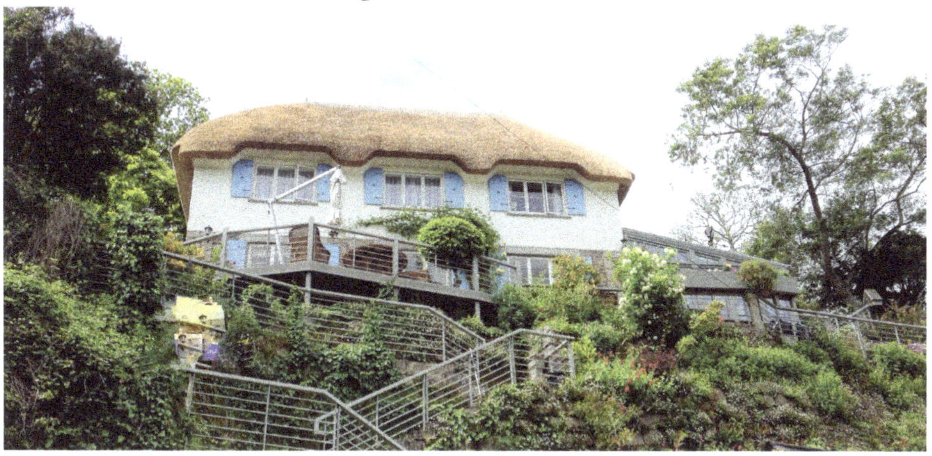
Stunning thatched cottages are everywhere to be seen.

Helford to Falmouth

This lovely section of the West Cornwall coastline starts by making its way in an easterly direction to head back out of the Helford River, where it passes by the delightful coastal hamlet of Durgan.

Next the coast passes around the dramatic scenery of Rosemullian Head which gives fantastic views across to the adjacent Bream Cove.

The little beach at Maenporth is a little further north, which is a fantastic place to spend the day soaking up the sun on a summers day. When you have warmed yourself up, then make your way down to the sea to dip your feet into the translucent water, which is always lapping up against the golden sand of this stunning cove.

As the coast edges a few miles north from the peace and tranquillity of Maenporth, the busier town of Falmouth comes into view, with the striking feature of Pendennis Castle standing proud upon the awe-inspiring Pendennis Point.

Falmouth has strong connections to the sea and its maritime history is rich and fascinating. This charming old seaside town is well worth visiting if you are lucky enough to find yourself in West Cornwall, where you will find lots to see and there are also plenty of attractions to go and enjoy. Coupled with beautiful views of the ocean and lots of excellent restaurants, this little hub of activity is a joy to behold.

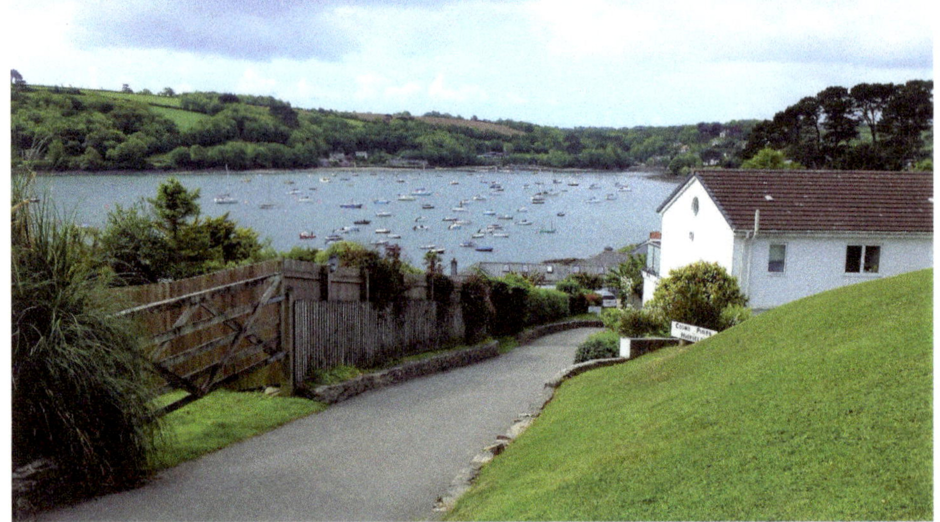

Looking across the beautiful Helford River from the hamlet of Durgan.

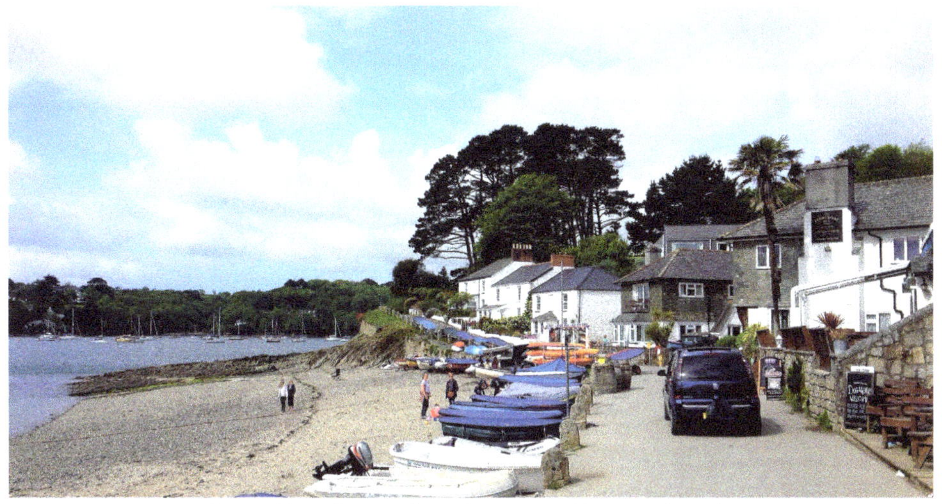
Boats line the sand at the pretty Durgan beach.

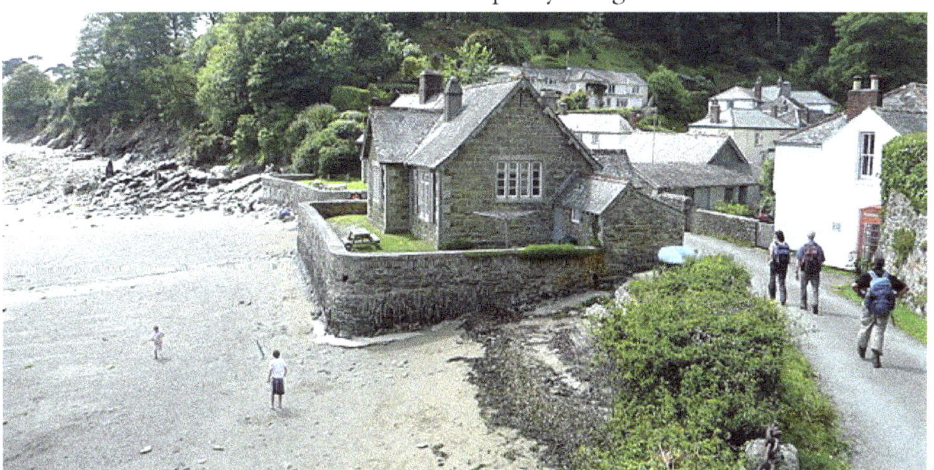
A room with a view, a cottage built on the banks of Helford River.

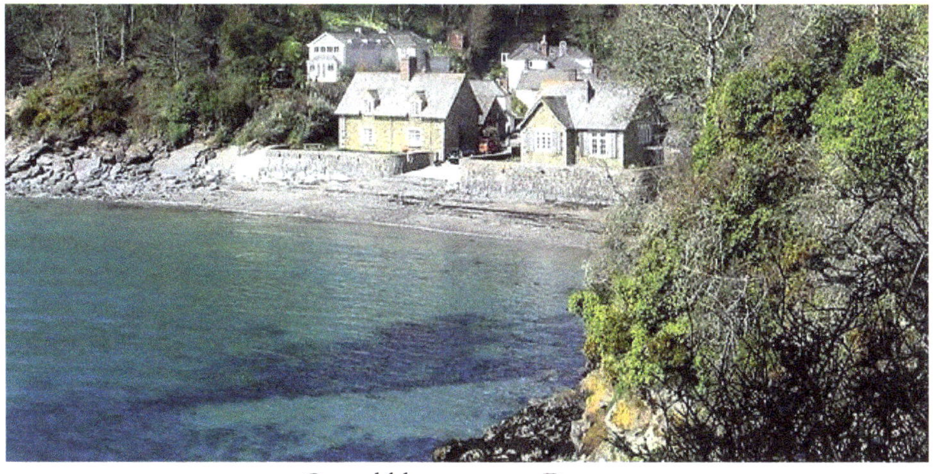
Crystal blue water at Durgan.

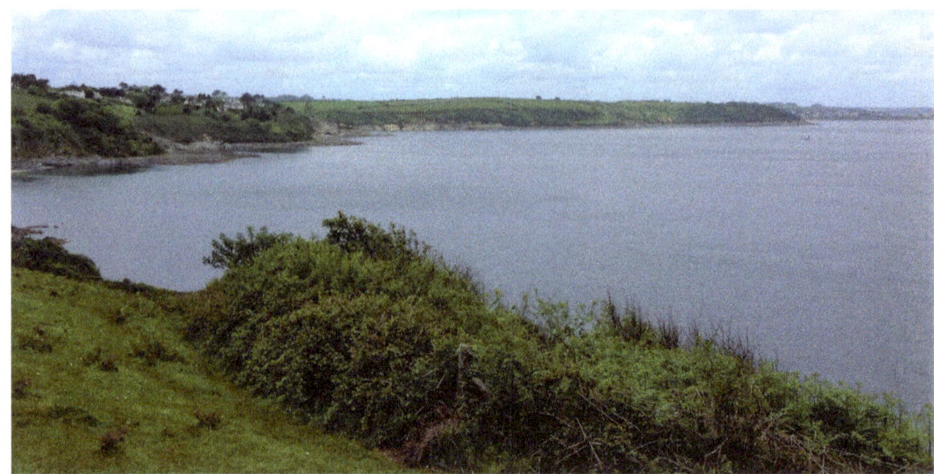

On the coastal path, looking north towards Rosemullian Head.

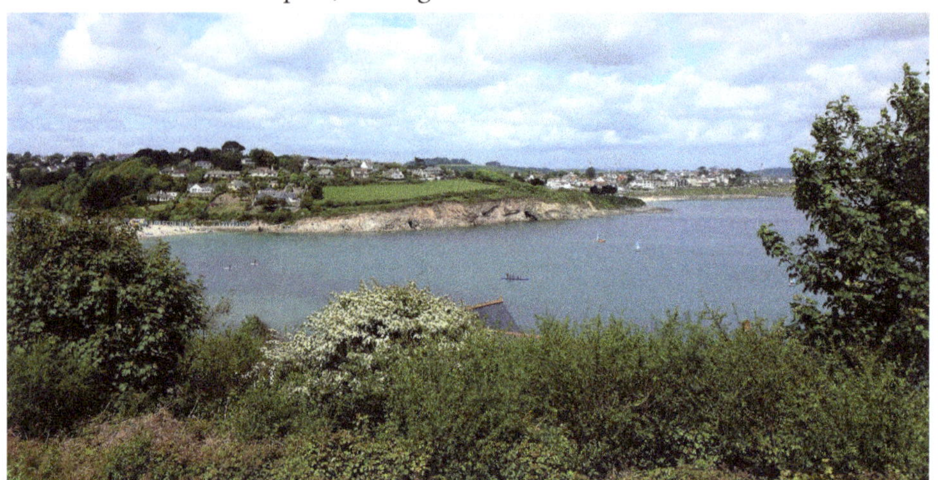

Stunning scenery from the coast path.

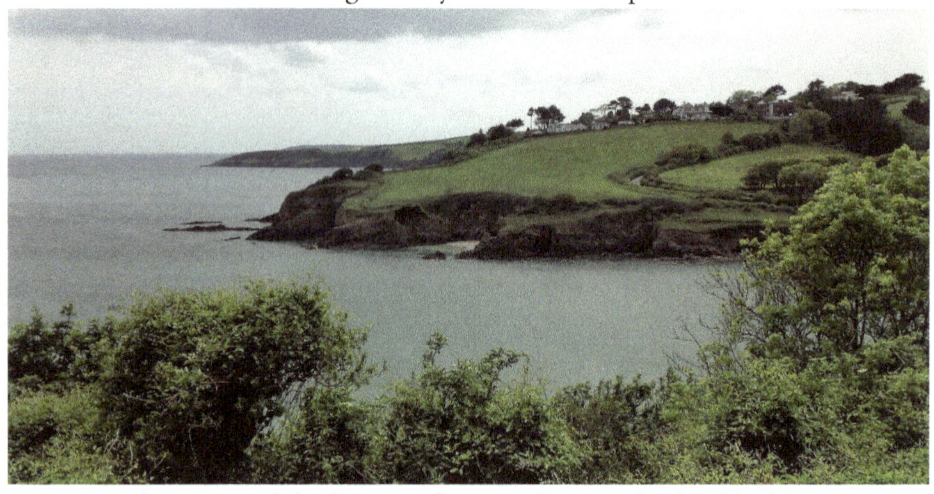

On the coast path looking south across the mouth of Helford River.

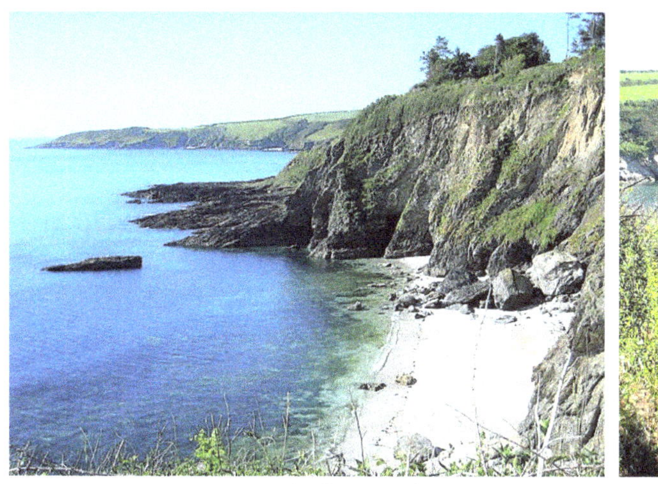
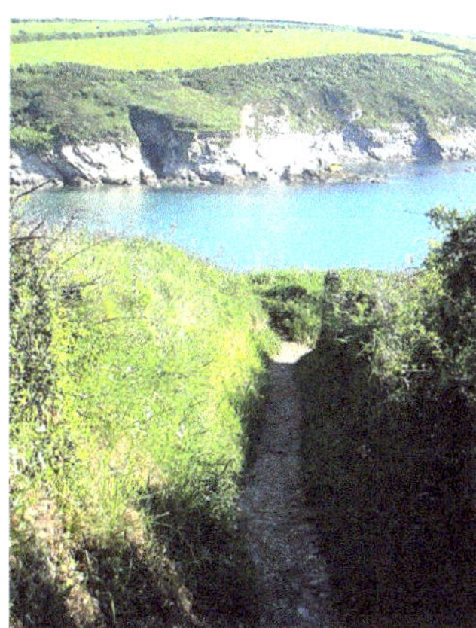
The beautiful setting of Maenporth.

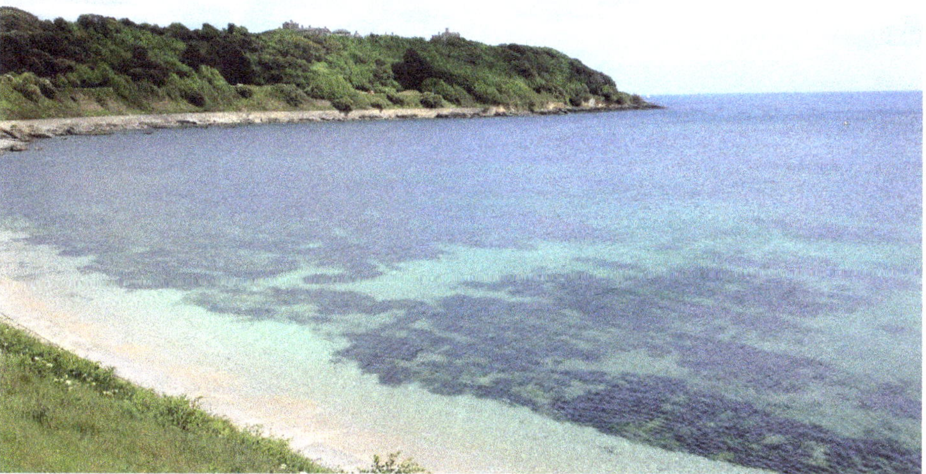
The idyllic Maenporth Beach.

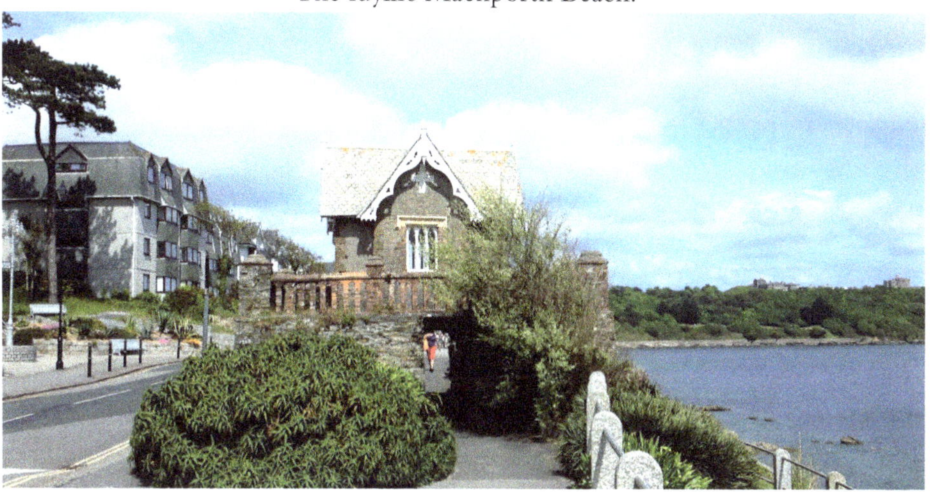
An unusual house that can be walked under, nearing Pendennis Point.

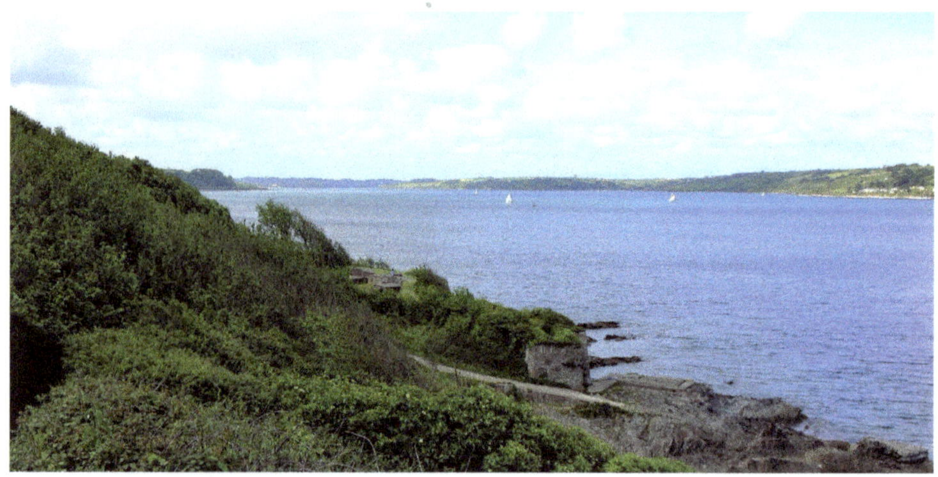

Beautiful scenes from the south west coast path near Falmouth.

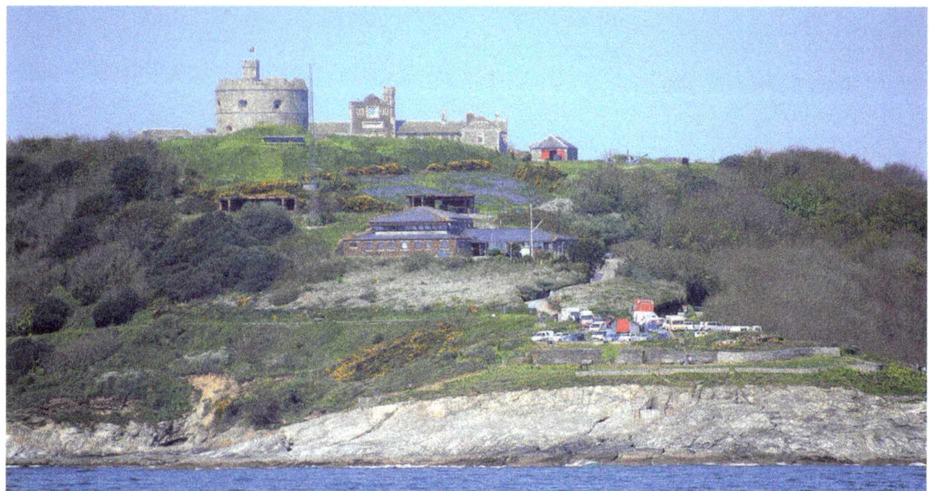

The majestic Pendennis Castle, on top of Pendennis Point.

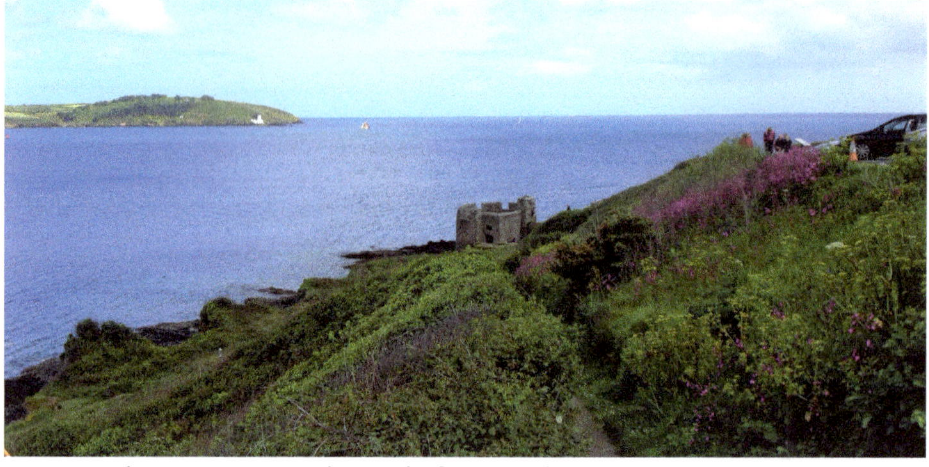

Looking across Carrick Roads, from Pendennis Point to Zone Point.

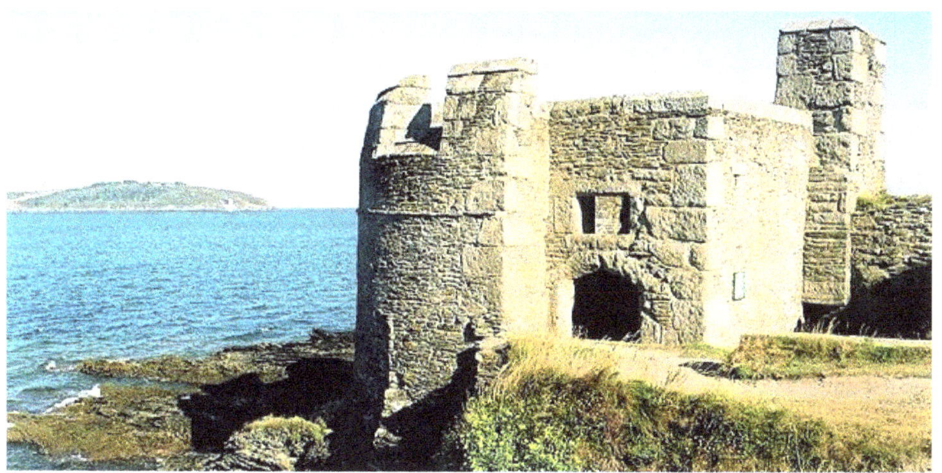
'The Blockhouse' on the headland of Pendennis Point.

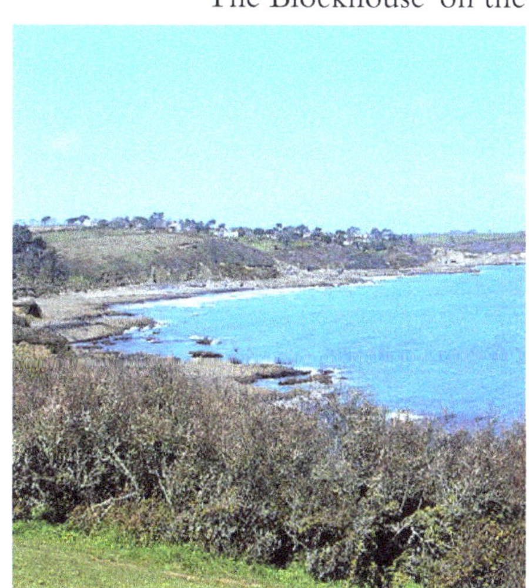
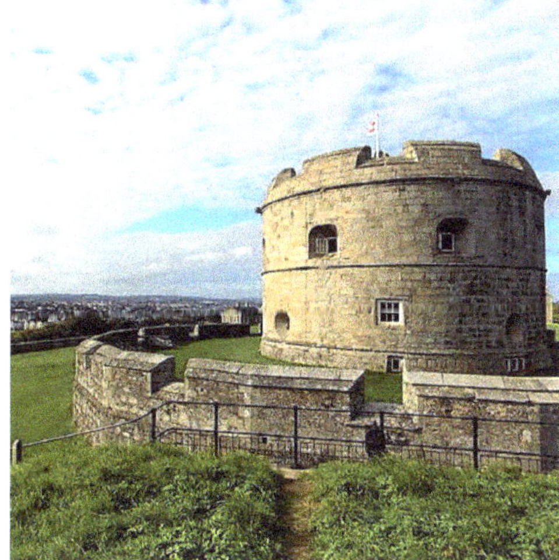
The coastline approaching Falmouth and (right) Pendennis Castle.

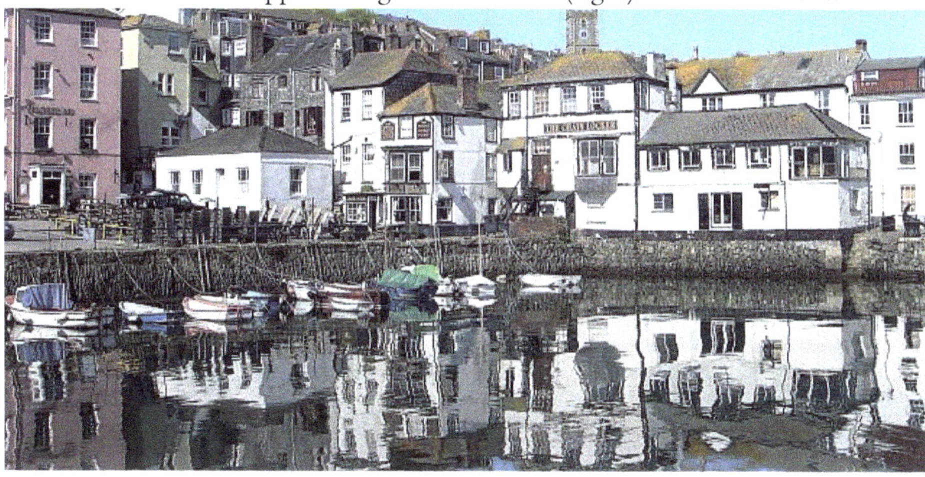
The picturesque Falmouth Harbour.

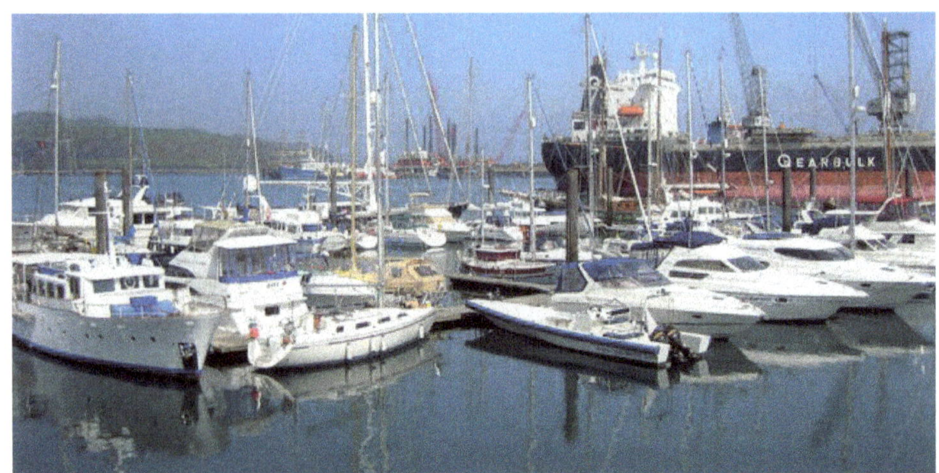

Boats moored at Falmouth Marina.

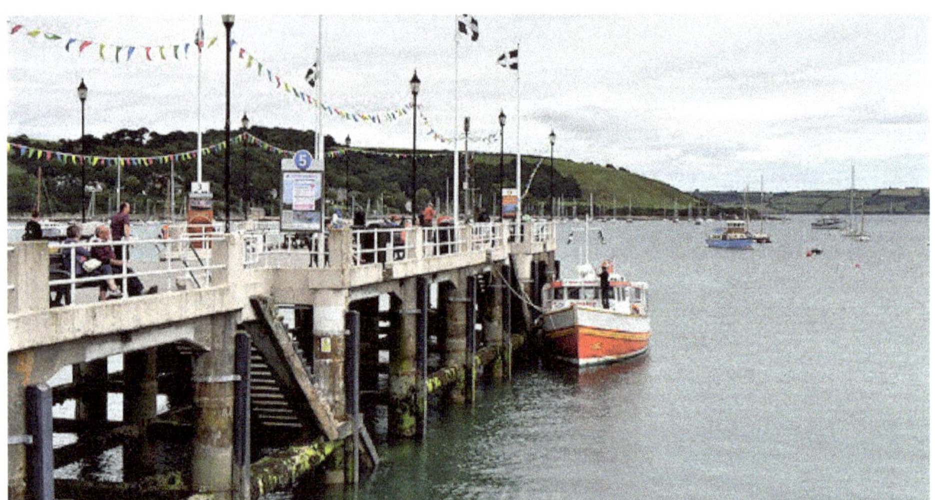

Boarding a ferry at Falmouth.

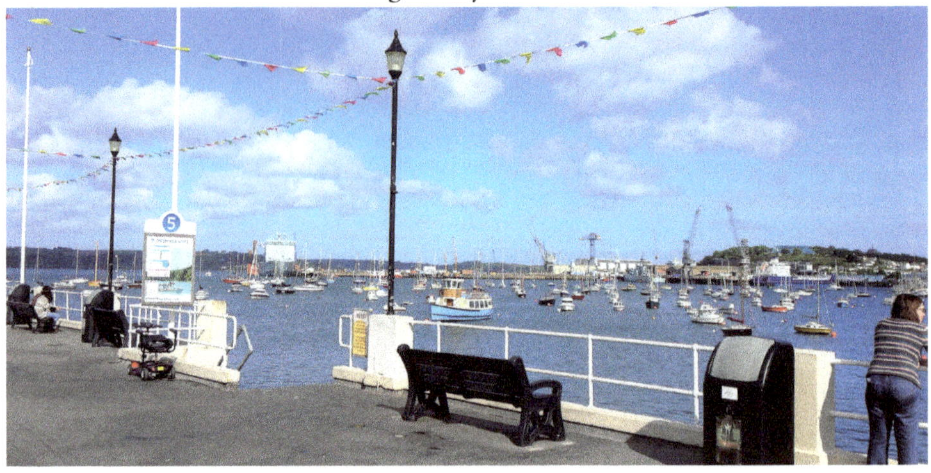

The picturesque Falmouth Harbour on a summers day.

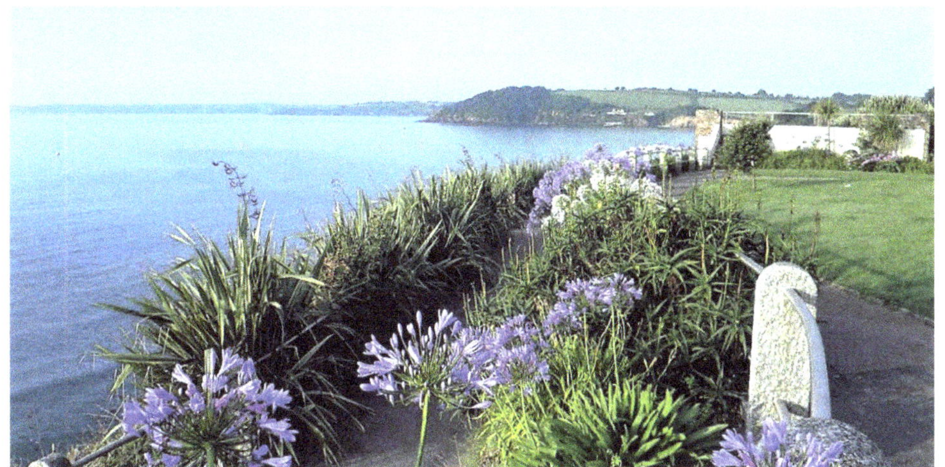

Flowers in bloom at Falmouth seafront.

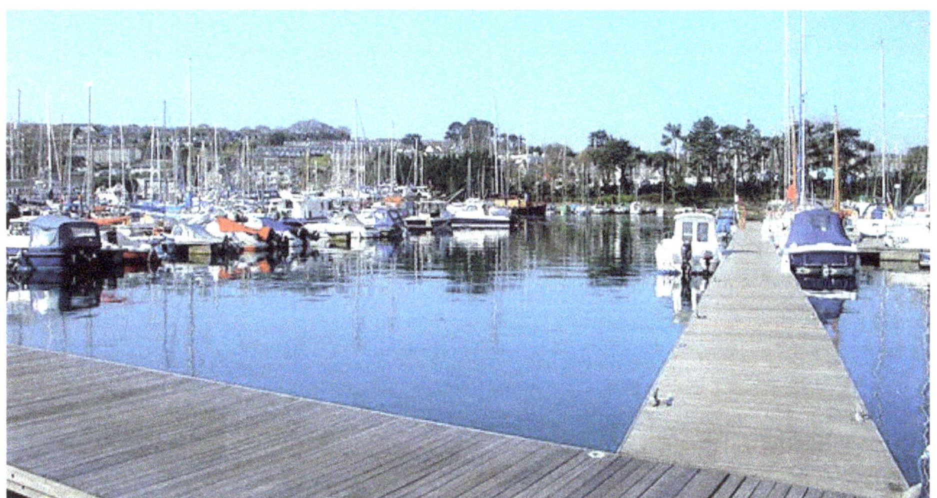

Yachts lined up at Falmouth Marina.

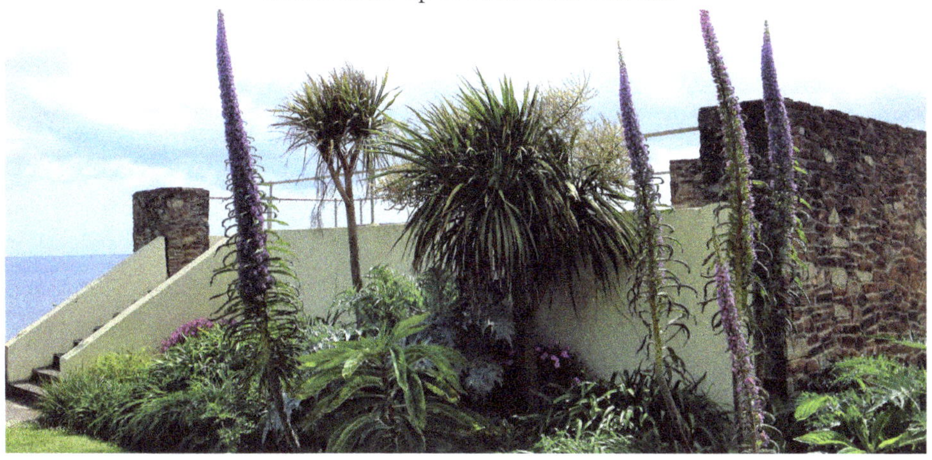

Echium's in full bloom at a garden near the seaside, Falmouth.

Photography Credits

All photography Copyright © S.V.P, apart from that listed below. (All photo's are licensed for reuse under Creative Commons Licenses CC by SA 2.0, and are the Copyright © of the persons stated below):
Front cover photo by © Benjamin Elliot on unsplash. Rear cover photo by © Angela Pham on unsplash. Page 2, Godrevy Lighthouse in 1949, geograph from David M Murray Rust. Page 5 bottom by Magda V on unsplash. Page 8 by Rumman Amin on unsplash. Contents Page bottom: Porthminster Beach St Ives, Angela Pham on unsplash.

Portreath to Godrevy Point: p10 Lighthouse: geograph by Jo Turner, p10 bottom: geograph by Alan Simkins, p11 top geograph by Tony Atkin, p11 middle geograph by G Laird, p11 bottom geograph by Joe Pritchard.
Godrevy Point to Hayle: p14 bottom by Lewis Clarke, p15 top by Ben Mitchell on unsplash, p15 middle by geograph David M Murray Rust, p15 bottom by Steven Haslington, p16 top by Peter Trimming, p16 middle by Mari Buckley.
Hayle to St Ives: p18 top geograph by Tim, p18 middle left by Andrew Abbott, middle right by geograph David M Murray Rust, p18 bottom geograph Alan Rolfe, p19 top geograph Alan Rolfe, p19 middle by Benjamin Elliott on unsplash, p19 bottom left by Andrew Ireand on unsplash, p20 top by Gary Rogers, p20 middle by Malcolm Lightbody on unsplash, p21 top by Simon Godfrey on unsplash, p21 middle by Tom Rickhuss on unsplash, p21 bottom right by Simon Godfrey on unsplash, p22 middle right by Simon Godfrey on unsplash, p23 middle left by geograph Steven Haslington, p23 bottom left by geograph Sarah Smith, p23 bottom right by geograph Graham Horn.
St Ives to Zennor: p25 bottom by geograph from David M Murray Rust, p26 top geograph by Graham Horn, p26 middle left by geograph by Chris Allen, p26 middle right by Philip Halling, p26 bottom left by Chris Downer, p27 top by Philip Halling, p27 middle geograph by Chris Downer, p27 bottom left by geograph Cornwall Guide.
Zennor to Pendeen: p28 top by geograph Jim Champion, p31 top by geograph Lewis Clarke, p31 middle by geograph Sarah Smith, p31 bottom left by geograph Mari Buckley, p31 bottom right by geograph Rude Health.
Pendeen to Cape Cornwall: p32 by Annie Spratt on unsplash, p33 top by geograph John Harrison, p33 middle left by geograph Guy Butler Madden, p33 middle right by Annie Spratt on unsplash, p33 bottom geograph Chris Gunns, p34 middle left by geograph Tony Atkin, p34 middle right by geograph Gareth James.
Cape Cornwall to Porthcurno: p37 bottom by Annie Spratt on unsplash, p38 top by Benjamin Elliott on unsplash, p39 middle by Benjamin Elliott on unsplash, p40 bottom by geograph Bill Boaden, p41 top by Magda V on unsplash, p41 middle by Charisse Kenion on unsplash.
Porthcurno to Marazion: p43 top by geograph Jim Champion, p43 middle left by Megan Andrews on unsplash, p43 middle right by geograph Rod Allday, p43 bottom by geograph Sarah Charlesworth, p44 top by geograph Bob Jones, p44 middle left by geograph Richard Knights, p44 middle right by geograph Pauline E, p44 bottom by geograph Sarah Charlesworth, p45 top by geograph Martin Bodman, p45 middle by Benjamin Elliott on unsplash, p45 bottom by Benjamin Elliott on unsplash, p46 top by Andrew Buchanan on unsplash, p46 middle left by geograph Claire Ward, p46 middle right by geograph Malcolm Brown, p46 bottom by Benjamin Elliott on unsplash, p47 top, middle by Benjamin Elliott on unsplash, p48 top by geograph Richard Johns, p48 middle left by geograph Hayley Green, p48 middle right by geograph Pam Brophy, p49 by Benjamin Elliott on unsplash.
Marazion to Porthleven: p51 top by geograph Lewis Clarke, p51 middle left by geograph Lewis Clarke, p51 bottom by geograph Philip Halling, p52 top by geograph Bob Jones, p52 middle by geograph Bill Boaden, p52 bottom by geograph Rod Allday, p53 top by geograph Philip Halling, p53 middle left by geograph Philip Halling, p53 bottom by geograph Bill Boaden, p54 top by geograph Mari Muckley, p55 middle left by geograph Rod Allday, p55 middle right by Pam Brophy, p55 bottom by geograph Philip Halling.
Porthleven to Lizard Point: p62 Kynance Cove by John Such on unsplash.
Helford to Falmouth: p81 middle by geograph by Graham Horn, p81 bottom by geograph Chris Johnson, p83 top left and right by geograph Rod Allday, p84 middle by geograph Lewis Clarke, p85 top by geograph Chris Downer, p85 middle left by geograph Trevor Harris, p85 middle right by geograph Chris Downer, p85 bottom by geograph Tony Atkin, p86 top by geograph Rod Allday, p86 middle by geograph David Dixon, p86 bottom by geograph, p87 top by geograph Steve Fareham, p87 middle by geograph Graham Loveland. Page 89 by Benjamin Elliot on unsplash.

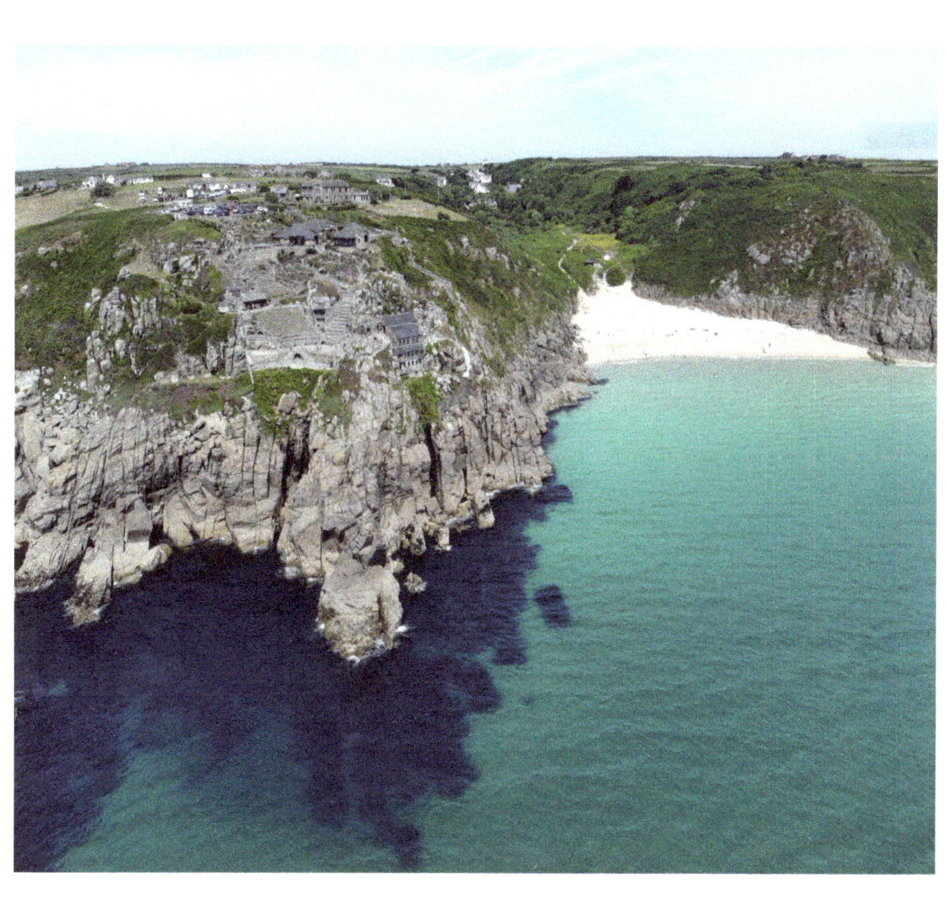

www.ingramcontent.com/pod-product-compliance
Ingram Content Group UK Ltd.
Pitfield, Milton Keynes, MK11 3LW, UK
UKHW062304290726
14090UKWH00017B/873

9 781739 293413